Farming in Wales
1936–2011

75 years
of the Farm Business Survey

Farming in Wales
1936–2011

Richard Moore-Colyer

Edited by Tony O'Regan

First impression: 2011

© Copyright Aberystwyth University and Y Lolfa Cyf., 2011

Editor: Tony O'Regan

Photographs: Richard Moore-Colyer, Alun Davies & Tony Pugh
Cover design: Howard Adair

ISBN: 978 184771 364 3

FSC

Published and printed in Wales
on paper from well maintained forests
by Y Lolfa Cyf., Talybont, Ceredigion SY24 5HE
website www.ylolfa.com
e-mail ylolfa@ylolfa.com
tel 01970 832 304
fax 832 782

In this light surely accounts may be said to be the foundation of good husbandry, and highly possible to convert a bad farmer into a good one... Many of them give in to unnecessary expenses, prosecute more experiments than their fortunes will admit, and bring themselves, by degrees, and unknowingly of the amount, into a want of money. A man that keeps regular accounts may certainly do the same; but he must infallibly know how much he expends, and be warned regularly of the danger; which are points of no slight importance.

J.M. Wilson, The Rural Cyclopedia (Edinburgh, 1849).

Worthy advice perhaps; yet by the third decade of the twentieth century the cheque book stub, the hastily-scribbled note in a daily diary, the bills stuffed at random in a desk drawer or behind the Swansea ware on the kitchen dresser, remained in many cases the predominant basis of farm accounting. The era of management via the proverbial 'back of the fag packet' may have been steadily waning, but had not yet drawn to its close...

Dedication and Acknowledgement

When the Farm Management Survey (the precursor of the Farm Business Survey) started it had five worthy objectives. These were:

be of services to agriculture and to the State in the framing of public policy in regard to the industry,

supplement official statistics by collecting information annually of the capital, equipment and labour employed, purchases of prerequisites and sale of produce,

ensure that an adequate picture of farming and of changes in output, costs, organisation and equipment exists,

enable cooperating farmers and others to increase their efficiency and to organise their farms on a more profitable basis, and

supply the means for local and national research into the main economic problems of the industry.

Since its inception the Survey has had a focus on business analysis at its very heart and for decades has provided the user of farm accounts with detailed information on which to base major spending decisions at farm, government and European Union level. It is recognised as the most authoritative survey of the financial position and performance of farm incomes, and its influence over the last 75 years cannot be oversold. Without it, the agricultural world would have been a darker and more ignorant place. That said, if the Survey is to celebrate its centenary, it must continue to be seen as vital for agricultural and rural policy makers not only in providing value for money, whatever that means, but also remaining relevant to the industry and its ever-evolving needs.

Aberystwyth University has been associated with land-based studies since 1878, and the Farm Survey is its oldest research contract. It is appropriate therefore, on behalf of the University, that I gratefully acknowledge the many farmers throughout Wales who have, for over three quarters of a century, generously made detailed business information available and also to the Welsh Assembly Government who finance the present Survey.

Finally, it would be remiss of me not to recognise the long list of past and present dedicated, highly skilled and talented individuals whom the University has had the pleasure and privilege of sending out onto farms to dig out the paper bags, scrutinise the ledgers and consume all the freshly baked biscuits and Welsh cakes, without whom, along with the farmers, no Survey would have been possible.

Tony O'Regan
Director of the Farm Business Survey

Contents

CHAPTER FOUR
The Origins of the Farm Business Survey

CHAPTER FIVE
The Development of the Survey, 1936–62

CHAPTER SIX
The Farm Business Survey – Towards the Present

CHAPTER SEVEN
The Survey as a Resource for Historians

CHAPTER EIGHT
Continuity and Change

List of Plates

Foreword

IT GIVES ME GREAT pleasure to write the foreword to *Farming in Wales 1936–2011*. Wales has a history punctuated by great people and traditions and for generations farmers have contributed to this history and it is imperative these contributions are recorded. This book helps safeguard the history of the countryside and rural way of life which are so important to Wales.

The world has certainly changed since 1936 and this book reminds us just how self-contained and self-sufficient we once were. It admirably portrays to present and future generations the hard times their forefathers endured in order to gain today's prosperity. They will realise the sacrifices they made and may encourage us all to acknowledge their contribution to our way of life. Hopefully this will result in all of us involving ourselves more in local activities and supporting our communities and the old traditions for the benefit of the nation as a whole.

This book chronicles the past three quarters of a century, bringing fond memories of a time gone by. Today's farming is largely run from Europe, not necessarily to the advantage of the Welsh farmer. European grants have kept the farming production line going, but these days money is also spent keeping the land out of production. But as you realise, once you read this book, farmers can't live on subsidies to keep vermin and trees!

This book will appeal to all and I hope that every farm, indeed every home in Wales will, in time, have a copy of *Farming in Wales 1936–2011* to reflect upon.

Dai Jones (Llanilar) MBE, FRAgS

Preface

INFORMATION IS MORE OR less essential to effective governance. From Tudor times onwards, administrations have sought to gather reliable data relating to national patterns of trade and the balance between exports and imports. Some idea of the webs of internal trade and, above all, the productivity of the land, was particularly vital in times of crisis. For this reason the government commissioned studies of the agriculture of the individual counties of Wales and England and arranged for the gathering of detailed county crop returns when Britain faced the real prospect of invasion from France in the late 1790s. Half a century later attempts were made to survey the farming of several counties and, in 1866, the first June 4th Returns were gathered. Meanwhile corn prices for Wales and England had been published in the *London Gazette* since 1772, although an official price series for livestock had to await the 1887 Markets and Fairs Act, after which livestock prices appeared in the annual *Agricultural Statistics of Great Britain*.

From the mid-nineteenth century various parliamentary investigations and Royal Commissions assembled data about the state of farms and the farming workforce, but it was only in the first half of the following century that systematic and comprehensive information gathering was developed in response to the need to manage and administer an increasingly complex sector of the economy. The evolution of the new science of statistics, led by R.A. Fisher, F. Yates, K. Pearson and others, allowed for the elaboration of sampling techniques which, in turn, paved the way for the scientific survey. As geographers like Dudley Stamp set about surveying land utilisation in Britain, so did Aberystwyth based R.G. Stapledon and his colleague William Davies produce their *Survey of the Agricultural and Waste Lands of Wales* in 1936.

Stamp, Stapledon and Davies's surveys allowed the authorities an overall glimpse of the land surface, but they revealed little of the economic condition of those who managed it. Most agricultural officials knew that many farmers in Wales and on the more marginal lands of England were having a hard time of it in the 1930s, but beyond the fact of rural depopulation, hard evidence was difficult to come by. Few farmers, after all, kept analysable sets of accounts. Some may have scribbled down cursory jottings of income and expenditure when the mood took them and others may have noted in their diaries details of yields obtained and prices received, but as a rule the vast majority had little real notion of the meaning and value of farm accounts. Farmers in Wales as well as England were generally content to see a positive balance in their bank books without being over-inquisitive as to the contribution of each enterprise on the farm to that balance.

To Welshmen in particular, the idea of a salaried official having the effrontery to question a man as to his financial affairs was anathema. Besides, farmers deeply distrusted officialdom. Officialdom had sold them down the river after the Great War and had left most of them exposed to the chilly blast of competition from cheaply-produced imports. Officialdom had done little to ameliorate the rural poverty of many parts of north and west Wales any more than it had acted to bring succour to the depressed areas of the industrial south. In any event, for an outsider to ask about their finances was seen by most farmers to be at best ill-mannered and, at worst, a preposterous imposition.

This book deals with the breakdown of the Welsh farmer's distrust of officialdom and his unwillingness to expose his financial affairs to external scrutiny. Against a background of change and development in Welsh farming over 75 years, it discusses the origin and evolution of the Welsh Farm Business Survey, its personnel, personalities and operation. The early pioneers managed somehow to persuade farmers to take part in the Survey and, with the passing of time and the development of the science of agricultural accounting, the reluctance of many farmers to attend to the business side of their activities gradually evaporated. The Survey soon became recognised by the authorities as a vital tool in strategic planning, and by farmers as a benchmark against which they could measure the success or otherwise of their enterprises. In celebrating the Farm Business Survey, the book also celebrates three quarters of a century of farming in Wales, focussing primarily upon the livestock sector. During this period the farmer's role in the countryside dramatically changed and farming is now no longer the straightforward business identified in the data gathered by the Survey's first investigational officers. Today's Welsh farmer faces physical, economic and psychological challenges which his forbears in 1936 would have found difficult to imagine.

The idea of producing a celebratory volume was first raised by Mr A. O'Regan, Director of the Welsh Farm Business Survey, in 2009. In compiling the volume I have frequently drawn upon the recollections and reminiscences of various people connected either directly or indirectly with the Survey, and these individuals will find themselves acknowledged in footnotes as appropriate. More generally I have benefitted from the advice and guidance of Professors D.I. Bateman and Michael Haines, Dr D.A.G. Green and Messers G.O. Hughes, David Williams, Rowland Davies, Nigel Chapman and Tony O'Regan himself. The farmers who generously gave of their time in allowing Dr Alun Davies or I to interview them are individually acknowledged in the final chapter of the book. They will readily recognise the photographs which they kindly allowed us to reproduce. It goes without saying that all errors and solecisms remain the responsibilty of myself or the editor.

Richard Moore-Colyer
June 2011

CHAPTER ONE

Farming in Wales between the Wars: an overview

Prelude

THE 1930s HAVE BEEN rightly described as a dark, dishonest decade, bringing untold misery to the depressed industrial areas of Britain and hardship, strife and fear to much of Continental Europe. However, the myth of unrelieved depression often associated with those sometimes turbulent years can no longer be sustained.[1] Various studies published over the last few years suggest that for the growing numbers of white-collar workers in Britain, real wages and standards of living tended to increase as the decade moved forward. For those actually in work, the sunlit uplands beckoned and the prospects of material betterment, holidays and even home ownership became increasingly real. Concurrently, demand for consumer goods forged ahead while a growing population demanded not only more variety in its diet, but looked for qualitative improvements.

The Labour Government of the 1920s had been reluctant to offer protection to the food and agricultural industry in the face of worldwide structural food surpluses.[2] But in 1931 the National Government, ignoring the anti-protectionist polemics of Beveridge and his followers, introduced a raft of measures embodying a built-in preference for Imperial primary products

19

on the British market. In so doing they embarked upon a journey which would finally draw to a close the long period of free trade initiated by the repeal of the Corn Laws in the mid-nineteenth century. The theoretical difficulties of reconciling the apparent incompatibility between protection and Imperial preference were circumvented by negotiating specific trade agreements. By these means the problematic circle was squared; home living costs were kept down at the same time as a gesture was made towards the farming interests.[3] This gradual abandonment of *laissez faire* policies was complemented by the Agricultural Marketing Acts of 1931 and 1933 under which marketing boards for milk, bacon, pigs and hops were eventually established. These broad policy changes, together with massive government investment in arterial drainage programmes, took place against a background of expanding agricultural education, major developments in plant and animal breeding and the first detailed studies of the chemistry and mode of action of a range of herbicides, pesticides and fungicides. The upshot was that the output of the agricultural sector of the economy increased by 27 per cent between 1920–2 and 1935–9, alongside a contraction of some 2.7 million acres in the farmed acreage.[4] Yet, despite the changing policies of the 1930s, the fact remains that by the outbreak of the Second World War, overseas sources still contributed 65 per cent of Britain's food supplies.

Taken overall, we must now see the interwar agricultural 'depression' very much as a regional and sub-sectoral affair with the strongly arable areas, including those of north-east Wales, the Glamorgan and Pembrokeshire lowlands and the lands of the English border, as being the principal sufferers under the earlier free trade policies.[5]

Another Land, Another Story

Wales entered the 1930s after a period of rural depression which had continued intermittently since the 1880s despite a few years of respite during the Great War. Unhappy landlord/tenant relations, chronic shortages of working capital and a profound suspicion of change had punctuated the Welsh farming world, while considerations of climate and terrain had severely limited both the types of farming practised and any potential for adopting technical developments.[6] Many farmers had purchased their holdings from their impoverished landlords in the immediate postwar years, so that owner/occupation level had advanced from 9 per cent in 1909 to 39 per cent by 1936. But this had little real effect on farming practice and age-old methods continued to be widely practised. There was about the Welsh countryside of the early 1930s a mild flavour of decay. The bald statistics reveal a melancholy picture of a unique web of national life beginning to rot at the centre. As rural population declined, with only Carmarthenshire, Denbighshire and Flintshire returning higher populations in 1931 than 1921, so the proportion of monoglot Welsh speakers began to collapse and Welsh gave way to English as the language of the Breconshire uplands and other parts of central and southern Wales.[7] At the same time, old traditions of craftsmanship and rural industry continued to decline and it seemed to many observers that the previously self-sufficient rural community was moving towards dissolution.[8] Such a dispiriting scenario could hardly fail to influence the attitudes of those for whom the land and the farm were the epicentres of social and cultural life. The closely knit and cohesive fabric of rural society, with its reciprocal duties and obligations, seemed frayed to the point of destruction and, as it appeared to slip away, it carried with it much of the quiet pride and satisfaction characteristic of localism. Perhaps it was a sense of the loss of a cherished past that prompted the 'make do and mend' and rather ramshackle approach to things characteristic of the countryside of much of Wales during the dark decade? After all, if no one particularly cared, why bother to spend a couple of hours mending a hedge with a billhook if a relict bedstead would do the job just as well? In any event, it is probably the case that economic circumstances alone do not entirely explain the creeping dereliction so deplored by R.G. Stapledon, T.J. Jenkin and others at the Welsh Plant Breeding Station at Aberystwyth.[9]

The arable area of Wales fell from 854,000 acres in 1915–19 to 571,000 acres in 1935–9 with a concomitant rise of half a million acres of rough grazing, more than a fifth of this being *Nardus/ Molina* moorland. Irrespective of the remarkable achievements of the Plant Breeding Station and the important contributions of both college and extramural teaching at the University Colleges of Aberystwyth and Bangor, the quality and productivity of most Welsh grasslands improved little in the decade before the Second World War.[10] Little attention was paid to drainage, bracken control or reseeding and, as weeds flourished in the soggy fields, lime deficiency steadily accumulated.[11] As noted by T.J. Jenkin, the land appeared unkempt and slovenly which, in his view, was entirely symptomatic of poor farming.[12] Jenkin, Moses Griffiths and others begged and cajoled farmers to visit the Plant Breeding Station at Aberystwyth to inspect some of its practically-based grassland experiments. Many recorded their gratitude and expressed admiration for all they had seen, yet, with some reason, they hesitated at the thought of investing scarce capital in pasture improvement merely to expand output in an already glutted market. The 1937 Agriculture Act with its offer of subsidies of 25 and 50 per cent to offset the cost of lime and basic slag had a modest effect, particularly on dairy holdings. In general, though, integrated programmes of pasture improvement were few and far between, so the grasslands of Wales continued to retain a distinctly neglected, weed infested and desolate appearance.[13]

Conservatism, indifference to material progress and bitterness at the gradual erosion of ancient traditions were all cited by contemporaries as being at least in part instrumental in the very limited progress of Welsh farming in the course of the interwar years. Paradoxically, though, a strong body of ruralist opinion took the view that the farming community of the more remote parts of Wales was somehow the depository of eternal truths and elemental wisdom worthy of saving. With their unique cultural heritage, these communities enshrined a traditional way of life which had much to teach the rest of society and, as such, they were deserving of protection against what many saw as the malignant forces of change.[14] Any attempt to rejuvenate them, it was felt, would need to be undertaken with sensitive reference to the complex interdependence between economy, society and culture.

But restoration and regeneration lay in the future. By the later 1930s, the economic situation as a whole was beginning to improve and agricultural prices began to move upwards, so that the bleak years of 1931–4 were merely an unhappy memory by 1936–7. Some farmers were now moving into an era of modest profits, although in many hundreds, if not thousands of cases, issues of terrain, accessibility and lack of public utilities prevented them from taking full advantage of the improved trading conditions. Of significance too was the deplorable state of rural housing the length and breadth of Wales, so much so that farmers, farm workers and labourers in the ancillary trades often subsisted under conditions deeply shocking to tourists and the medical authorities alike.

The much admired old farmhouses of Pembrokeshire and Breconshire, the vales of Clwyd and Glamorgan and the half-timbered country houses of the English border stood in stark contrast to those of the western and remote northern counties. (Plate 1) Reports by Sanitary Inspectors and Medical Officers of Health for Cardiganshire, for example, reveal a countryside

Plate 1. A Breconshire farmyard, c.1940

of damp, dank dwellings, their floors sodden, their gable ends sagging and their ill-fitting windows rattling in the wind. These places were the breeding grounds for disease, and diphtheria, pneumonia, tuberculosis and scabies were commonplace in the early decades of the last century. The extraordinarily enlightened Housing (Rural Workers) Act of 1926, which was continued by way of enabling legislation until 1945, offered some help by providing grants to property owners to enable them to create habitable dwellings from what were often little more than rural slums. Even so, the quality of rural housing stock in counties like Cardigan, Carmarthen, Merioneth and Caernarvon continued to remain extremely poor for many years.[15]

The improvement to farm incomes in the 1960s and 1970s allowed for the continued upgrading of farmhouses in terms of basic amenities and comforts. Yet, this often took place at the expense of the disfigurement of traditional lime washed buildings. Stone walls were rendered in concrete, Welsh slate roofs were replaced with tiles and, in extreme cases, the old house was abandoned in favour of a new construction or a roadside bungalow. If the rural slums disappeared, they were sometimes replaced with structures which, for all their comfort and convenience, were of questionable aesthetic merit. As the older cottages and farmhouses slipped further into decrepitude there was a tendency for them to be sold off to incomers eager to establish a foothold in the countryside. These unwanted dwellings were often lovingly renovated by enthusiasts with a keen awareness of the importance of the aesthetics of site and of the vital need to keep faith with traditional design and building materials.[16]

But above all else the farmhouses and cottages of the earlier period were dark, and once the sun had gone down there was little alternative but the 'Aladdin' paraffin lamp or the guttering candle. The various private electricity companies like the West Cambrian Power Company and the North and South Wales Power companies were certainly extending their coverage with the latter increasing the length of its transmission cables from 110 to 1,077 miles between 1925 and 1935. On the whole, though, these developments were only of benefit to urban customers so that by 1939, a mere 8 per cent of Welsh farms were linked to a public source of electricity. Others, of course, had their own petrol driven generators. In Carmarthenshire, for example, the 1941 National Farm Survey revealed that of the 10 per cent of all farms using electricity, nine out of ten generated their own supplies. Numerous contemporary studies and reports published in the *Welsh Journal of Agriculture* and elsewhere underlined the great benefits to farmers of rural electrification, especially in terms of barn machinery operation and of reducing the costs of milk production. Yet progress was slow, and if 30 per cent of Glamorgan farms were connected to public electricity supplies by 1941, the comparable figure for Cardiganshire, Anglesey, Radnorshire and Montgomeryshire was a mere two per cent.[17] Even where farms were connected and the electric light found its way into the farmhouse, electrical white goods remained relatively rare in the pre-war Welsh country kitchen. Farmers' wives, it seems, were happy to keep faith with their cast iron range, only turning to electricity (perhaps by way of the Baby Belling cooker which was selling for £4 in 1935) when cooking temperatures needed to be carefully controlled.[18]

Despite the slow diffusion of public electricity supplies and the equally slow rate of uptake on Welsh farms due mainly to economic factors, most people no doubt appreciated the enormous practical benefits of being able to obtain illumination at the flick of a switch. Besides, there were additional and perhaps more subtle advantages offered by the availability of a source of clean, safe and reliable power. In the sense that a farmer could go about his winter farm tasks with reduced fear of stumbling in the darkness or of missing some vital husbandry detail in the encircling gloom, the electric light offered a tremendous psychological boost. And if the electric motor helped reduce the input of physical effort to many farmyard tasks, one might suggest, without stretching the point too far, that it went some way towards promoting domestic harmony. If a man could complete his work rather earlier in the day, walk into his kitchen without being totally exhausted and enjoy the company of his wife and family for a few hours of the evening, an essential element of his home life would be fulfilled. A stable and contented home life would become even more important in the years ahead as numbers of farm servants and labourers declined and farmers became increasingly reliant on the input of their wives.[19] In 1926 Welsh farmers employed 62,364 servants and day labourers but within two decades the labouring population had fallen by ten thousand so that in effect many farmers were spending much of their time working alone. On a lonely and isolated upland farm where a man might work for days on end without company, a convivial domestic life was of the highest importance. Electricity, by easing his lot in barn and byre, and that of his wife in the home, may have gone some way towards promoting it.

Animals and the Economy of the Farm

Electricity, of course, had enormous potential to improve the lot of the livestock farmer. By 1936 livestock and livestock products comprised 90 per cent of the volume of output of Welsh farms with 70 per cent of total farm capital being invested in livestock compared to 8 per cent in crops and 17 per cent in implements and tools. Seventy five years ago there were almost 40,000 breeding sows in Wales, most of them concentrated in Flintshire, Denbighshire, Glamorgan and Carmarthenshire whence their fattened offspring found their way to the butchers of the adjacent industrial areas. But if pig production and the sale of eggs and poultry were locally important, the overwhelming contribution to livestock output came from cattle, sheep and milk. (Plate 2)

The Livestock Marketing Act of 1937 enabled growing numbers of finished animals to be despatched to abattoirs for sale on a dead weight basis, yet the great majority of cattle

Plate 2. Recently sheared sheep in Breconshire, *c*.1940

continued to be sold as stores so that farmers had little alternative but to engage with the anarchic and even shambolic store cattle market, with its irregular and unreliable prices. Many of the problems confronting the marketing of cattle were paralleled in the sheep sector, which was of major significance to the hill farm and of growing importance in the lowland. Efforts to promote pedigree recording and flock improvement, sponsored by the Welsh Mountain Sheep Breeders' Association and underpinned by Ministry of Agriculture grants channelled through local breed improvement societies, had led to steady qualitative improvements. In addition, a combination of increased hay yields on the more progressive farms, coupled with the availability of cheap imported concentrate feeds for cattle, had allowed for a modest degree of intensification of sheep on the lowland grassland/arable holding.[20] This was further facilitated by a decline in the numbers of two and three year old wethers in the face of growing public demand for smaller cuts from younger, leaner lambs.[21] While mutton continued to be produced in the uplands of Merioneth, Radnor and Breconshire, sheep producers in all but the most extreme hill country would soon direct their efforts towards the fat lamb trade.[22] Overall the breeding ewe population had reached 2.06 million by 1936, giving a total of some 4.4 million sheep, a ratio of five sheep for every head of cattle in Wales. As would prove to be the case many decades later, the reduction in the relative proportion of cattle on the hills amplified difficulties in pasture management and facilitated the insidious spread of bracken and a host of grass species of low nutritional value.[23]

But by no means was all doom and gloom. As arable acreage contracted after the Great War, oat production for on-farm consumption came to comprise 70 per cent of Welsh arable output by 1939, while green crop cultivation concurrently expanded consonant with the rapid development of dairy farming after

1933.[24] In Pembrokeshire, meanwhile, where pioneering work on the early crop undertaken by the county agricultural organiser, W.E.D. Jones, was beginning to bear fruit, potato production became of major importance in the farming economy by the mid-1930s.[25] At a local level, the husbandry of horticultural and market garden crops were offered encouragement with the passing of the Horticultural Produce (Emergency Customs Duties) Act of 1931. Sheltered valleys on the coastal belt, blessed with a mild climate and a burgeoning tourist trade were ideal for the purpose, and the seaside town of Aberystwyth, for example, received regular supplies of locally grown peas, carrots and brassicas during the summer season.[26]

These were but minor developments when compared with the expansion of the dairy sector, the economic salvation of a great many Welsh farmers by the later 1930s. Traditionally, the bulk of Welsh milk had been converted into butter and packed in casks for sale in the southern industrial valleys. During the first quarter of the twentieth century however, breast feeding of children became less common and, as tea drinking was established as an almost universal habit among all classes, there was a quantum increase in the demand for liquid milk.[27] Naturally protected from overseas competition, and appreciated more and more for its nutritional qualities, liquid milk seemed to offer major opportunities for farmers, particularly after the establishment of the Milk Marketing Board provided a guaranteed outlet for registered producers.

The provisions of the Milk and Dairies Order of 1908, the work of the newly-established National Institute for Research in Dairying and the activities of government-funded bacteriologists had significantly reduced the human health problems associated with milk drinking, and consumers were no longer mortally afraid of what had once been termed 'liquid dynamite'. Locally, the pioneering work of the peripatetic teachers and advisors from the dairy school in the basement of the Old College at Aberystwyth

The Long

VERSUS

The Short Haul

A great number of babies get their food through a tube many miles in length.

It often takes a day and a half for the milk to run from the cow end of the tube to the baby end of the tube.

This tube is open in many places and baby's food is frequently polluted. It is often wrongly kept in over-heated places.

There may be a diseased cow at the country end of the tube.

And yet some People Wonder Why So Many Babies Die!

On the other hand the mother-fed baby gets its milk fresh, pure and wholesome—no germs can get into it.

To Lessen Baby Deaths let us have More Mother-Fed Babies

You can't improve on Nature's Plan.

For your Baby's Sake Nurse It

Copies of the above as a Poster enlarged to 16¾ by 10¾ inches, mounted on a stiff card, varnished and with cord to hang, price 2/6; in leaflet form as this, price 3/- per 100, or 6d. per dozen *(half price to Members)*, postage extra: can be had on application to the Hon. Secretary:

THE NATIONAL CLEAN MILK SOCIETY (INCORPORATED),

2, SOHO SQUARE, LONDON, W. I.

Plate 3. National Clean Milk Society promotional material

had awakened farmers to the importance of 'clean milk production' as a means of reducing the incidence of coliform diseases and tuberculosis, the traditional bugbears of milk drinkers. (Plate 3)

Throughout the British Isles tuberculin testing and the production of graded milk of low bacterial count had been widely accepted and facilitated by the evolution of efficient on-farm cooling methods and numerous advances in machine milking technology.[28] With an eye to the main chance, farmers adjusted to the challenges of dairying and by 1930 three-quarters of all milk produced in England and Wales was marketed in liquid form. Within six years, 80 per cent of the liquid milk yielded by the 336,000 dairy cows in Wales was being despatched to one of the many cooperatively operated creameries up and down the country. The four counties of north Wales, for example, were served by no less than thirty creameries catering for farms in remote and inaccessible areas whose occupiers would not previously have considered dairying as a viable option.[29] On Anglesey no more than half a dozen farmers sold milk to the mainland in the 1920s, but with the opening of a cooperative creamery in Bangor in 1934 an important marketing opportunity presented itself. Aided by increasingly sophisticated motor lorries, two hundred of Anglesey's registered producers were sending milk to the Bangor outlet by 1939. As they did so, they were taking advantage of the newly formed Milk Marketing Board's pool pricing arrangements which enabled them to abandon seasonal production in favour of level output. The establishment of the Bangor creamery significantly changed the face of farming on Anglesey. Henceforth, many farmers shifted away from the traditional systems of store cattle raising and butter making and devoted themselves to dairying, with all that that implied for their working routines and social activities.[30] (Plate 4)

But alongside these dynamic marketing initiatives there remained the small producer retailer with his milk float and hand

Plate 4. The producer retailer, Mr Edmunds of Green Yard Farm, near Barry

cart. Usually located on the periphery of the larger towns, these small producers would typically have a herd of five to ten cows whose milk they would deliver from door to door. Irrespective of whether they plied their trade in Cardiff and Neath, Bangor or Llandudno, these men were regarded rather sniffily by the pundits, who felt that their habits, demeanour and appearance gave milk production a bad name. In fact, many looked forward to the day when pricing arrangements and competition would drive these small men 'of inadequate knowledge' back to other systems of farming.[31] Criticism of the producer–retailer was directed in the main at what were perceived to be generally poor standards of hygiene arising from ignorance of, or at best indifference to, modern methods of milk production. Other observers extended their criticism to embrace the Welsh dairy farming sector in general. There may, after all, have been a consistent diminution in the bacterial counts of milk sold from Welsh farms, yet of the 11,000 accredited (i.e. inspected and deemed bacteriologically satisfactory) dairy farms in Wales and England in 1935, only 896 were in Wales herself.[32] Inertia, it was averred, still ran deep. Breed improvement was widely neglected, housing of dairy animals was inadequate and on many farms little intention was paid to installing efficient cooling and sterilising equipment so that dairy management often remained crude and unhygienic. The first milking machine in Wales had been installed at Blaenant, Newcastle Emlyn in 1917. The event was something of an occasion in the Teifi valley, yet the diffusion of the milking machine throughout the rest of the country was very slow. There are no reliable statistics for earlier periods, but since there were a mere 3,649 milking machines in Wales in 1946, it would seem that the overwhelming majority of Welsh dairy cows continued to be milked by hand throughout the years leading up to the Second World War.[33] Critics also complained that farmers had failed to engage with the important business of milk recording, a vital key to establishing quantitative data to aid breed and herd improvement.[34]

Since genetic improvement can only be properly expressed under a suitable nutritional regime, much attention had been directed by advisors and teachers towards the importance of good grassland management and utilisation on the dairy farm. Many producers, though, were indifferent to their importuning. There seemed, after all, little point in going to the trouble and expense of grassland renovation when imported starches and proteins were available at rock-bottom prices. So it was that as late as 1938 some 60 per cent of starch equivalent and 72 per cent of protein equivalent fed to Welsh cows was derived from concentrated feeds.[35] The era of milk production from intensively-managed grassland with concentrates as an adjunct would have to await the postwar years.[36] (Plate 5)

However inefficient and obscurantist some of its producers may have been, milk offered a lifeline to hard-pressed Welsh farmers in the 1930s. Underpinned by a stable pricing and marketing system, milk sales provided a regular income, while the demands

Plate 5. Loading churns onto the milk train at Carmarthen

of twice-daily milking imposed the need for time management and the careful planning of work routines. In so doing it probably helped to create among many farmers a mindset suited to dealing with the dynamic events of the postwar years.

Horses and Machines

In May 1929, a reporter with the *Cardigan and Tivy-side Advertiser* filed a piece covering a demonstration of the new International Farmall tractor held at Synod Inn, Cardiganshire.[37] Although the event caused "a great stir", these early machines with their iron wheels, questionable reliability and thirst for off-farm inputs impressed few Welsh farmers so that there were a mere 1,932 tractors in Wales by the outbreak of the Second World War. So it was that the horse remained the primary source of tractive power on Welsh farms with more than 179,000 of these animals being recorded in the Agricultural Returns for 1936. Shires, Clydesdales and Welsh Cobs of various descriptions had been steadily improving in conformation and scope since the 1914 Livestock Improvement Scheme had provided grant aid to subsidise the stud fees of travelling stallions from beyond the local area.[38] Working horses, though, were expensive to keep, profligate in the use of land and, for much of the year, substantially underutilised. At peak periods of springtime cultivation and during haymaking they were constantly at work, but for the rest of the year, apart from autumn ploughing, root crop hauling and dung carting, they ate steadily and worked only sporadically. Nevertheless they remained indispensable both for local travel and for farm work. Arable acreage may have declined between the wars, yet the increased use of horse drawn hay mowers, turners and tedders and the need to shift bulky root crops for other livestock during the winter months ensured the horse's continued role on Welsh farms.[39]

Many people looked upon the horse as a tried and trusted companion, offering, through myth and legend, a link to an imagined past, to a world of gods and heroes. How could the tractor replace such a superb symbol of power and potency? Besides, horse work was men's work, and highly prized men's work at that! The Austin and Fordson tractors at the Royal Welsh Show of 1929, like the various commercial vehicles exhibited at shows throughout the 1930s may have been symbolic of the evolutionary process of the mechanisation of the farmstead, but for the time being they were little more.[40] It was true that the tractor created the potential for flexibility and more effective timeliness of husbandry operations, but farmers in Wales were suspicious of investing capital in machines carrying high annual depreciation charges. Besides, before the invention of the three-point linkage system in 1934–5, their working range was strictly limited. To the majority of farmers, the tractor was regarded as a costly irrelevance, and it only became an irresistible force in Welsh farming in the later years of the Second World War.

Mixed Fortunes

The pioneering work of the Aberystwyth-based economist J. Pryse Howell offers a valuable glimpse of the variable financial fortunes of Welsh farms during the challenging years of the 1930s. Howell undertook detailed yearly surveys of 60 Welsh farms, in excess of 20 acres in size, with the objective of ascertaining fluctuations in farm income on four general classes of holding as in Table 1 below.[41] Since the number and size of farms in different categories varied each year, direct annual comparisons are of limited value although transposing the figures to a per 100-acre basis allows for some meaningful comparisons of temporal changes in income on what were generally undercapitalised holdings. The average capital deployed per 100 acres between 1925 and 1934 was as follows: Cattle and Sheep (Poor Land) £388; Cattle and Sheep (Better Land) £815; Mixed Farms £917; Cattle/Dairy £1,153. Some indication of the contribution to incomes from different sectors, derived from Howell's data, appears in Table 2.

Table 1. Farm incomes in £ per 100 acres on Welsh Farms, 1929–39.[42] (Figures in brackets represent negative incomes)

Years	Cattle & Sheep (Poor Land)	Cattle & Sheep (Better Land)	Mixed farms (Mainly Lowland)	Cattle / Dairy
1929–30	80	122	70	351
1930–1	56	152	87	168
1931–2	(4)	(20)	36	140
1932–3	(18)	5	(50)	68
1933–4	27	0	8	168
1934–5	32	44	260	163
1935–6	36	87	178	240
1936–7	58	54	211	130
1937–8	54	74	189	221
1938–9	12	3	131	239

Table 2. Percentage sector receipts on Welsh Farms of various sizes, 1929–38.

Output	Under 50 acres	51-99 acres	100-149 acres	Over 150 acres
Cattle	13.9	19.5	26.9	27.3
Dairy Products	35.4	37.8	27.0	23.9
Sheep and Wool	5.4	13.0	17.9	20.4
Pigs	22.4	10.8	12.3	14.3
Poultry and Eggs	18.0	10.3	5.4	5.0
Horses	0.6	1.7	3.1	3.1
Crops / Sundries	3.3	6.9	7.4	6.0

In all cases livestock and livestock products yielded in excess of 90 per cent of output with sales of pigs and poultry/eggs representing a disproportionately high component on the smaller farms.[43] The livestock producer in general weathered the difficult years of the early and mid-1930s more successfully than his arable brethren, yet Table 1 leaves little doubt as to the financial realities confronted by Welsh farmers in most sectors during this period. The Ministry of Agriculture's index of farm prices fell from 126 in 1929–30 to 86 in 1933–4. At the same time feed and fertiliser costs declined by a modest 10 per cent, while labour costs soared to 70 per cent above the levels prevailing during the Great War. This explains why, in the broadest of terms, the best returns were obtained on those farms with the lowest proportion of tillage crops and the minimum of hired labour.[44] Notwithstanding gradual, if fluctuating improvement as the decade advanced, the fact remains that on the two categories of sheep and cattle farms, income averaged a derisory four shillings per week per 100-acres between 1931 and 1934. This contrasts with 48 shillings and 60 shillings on mixed and cattle/dairy holdings, the fortunes of the former group being dependent upon producing a high proportion of output in the form of store or finished cattle or animals suited as replacements in dairy herds. Warts and all, Welsh farmers who concentrated their efforts on dairying seem to have survived the 1930s as effectively as anyone working the land.

CHAPTER TWO

Wartime Interlude

Farming for Victory

THE STORY OF BRITISH farming during the Second World War has been conventionally portrayed as one of selfless heroism. As ships carrying food to our shores were sent to the bottom of the Atlantic by German U-boats, supplies of imported foods fell by 85 per cent of pre-war levels and there was a real possibility of the country being starved into submission long before a single enemy soldier crossed the English Channel. Yet, in a Herculean enterprise, unparalleled in modern times, farmers and land workers threw their shoulders to the wheel and by their efforts, the nation was fed and morale was maintained. Over a period of six years, we are told by the official historian, an undercapitalised and poorly-equipped body of farmers transferred a rundown countryside into a productive farmscape.[1]

More recently this heroic scenario has been challenged, and there is now emerging a consensus view that the overall increase in agricultural productivity during the war was less impressive than the orthodox wisdom and propaganda suggests.[2] Furthermore, the much-vaunted technical advances alleged to have occurred during the war itself seem, on balance, to have been limited to mechanisation and the adoption of *existing* technology. In reality, the great technological revolution in farming did not occur until the early postwar decades and there were no significant yield improvements between 1939 and 1945. In terms of volume, British agricultural output increased by 8 per cent between 1935–9 and 1943–5 due, principally, to a dramatic expansion in the arable acreage at the expense of livestock production. Much of this change was stimulated by official pressure, advancing prices and a steep increase in the volume of inputs.[3]

But no revisionist writings can obscure the extraordinary changes to the farmscape wrought by wartime conditions. The Agriculture Act of 1939 left little doubt as to the government's determination to maximise national food output by giving every encouragement to farmers to expand both output and income. The Act confirmed the various subsidies on lime and slag established in 1937 and, along with other incentives, introduced the so called 'plough-up' grant of £2 per acre. So successful was this move that during the first season of the war, 2 million extra acres of arable land was created from permanent pasture. By the end of 1944, when farm prices had risen by 67 per cent above pre-war levels, an additional 4.5 million acres of pasture had been ploughed for arable. To facilitate the plough-up campaign, the Ministry of Agriculture embarked upon a massive programme of fertiliser and feedstuffs procurement, concurrently buying large quantities of farm machinery, much of it from the United States. This equipment was used in a series of nationwide reclamation schemes, besides being put at the disposal of farmers as they strove to meet their cultivation quotas. The Ministry itself owned no less than 10,600 tractors at the end of the war while the number of tractors owned by farmers in Wales and England increased from 56,200 in 1939 to 203,400 in 1946.[4]

Fighting Fascism with Fascism?

Several recent commentators have endorsed the view of the Aberystwyth-based economist and sociologist A.W. Ashby who argued that the expansion in the wartime output of crops and livestock products would probably have occurred naturally as a consequence of favourable economic circumstances. At the time, though, official propaganda held that much of the success of the war effort on the Home Front arose from the tight control of the farming industry (if not the rural world more generally), maintained by the County War Agricultural Executive Committees, the so-called 'Warags'. These bodies, declared the Ministry of Information, energised the countryside and mobilised farming to struggle for the common good. They were, the public was told, "… the most successful examples of decentralisation and the most democratic use of control that this war has produced".[5]

Established under the Emergency Powers (Defence) Act of 1939, the Warags were *appointed* bodies with no specific legal constitution, their unpaid members working alongside salaried technical staff to coordinate virtually all matters relating to food production on the Home Front.[6] At the county level, the numerical makeup of the different committees varied widely, often in accordance with the success or otherwise of Executive Officers in avoiding administrative overheads and strangulation with 'red tape'. Breconshire, for example, had an executive of 15 members who oversaw District Committees serving Devynock, Brecon, Builth and Talgarth. The District Committees, meanwhile, were kept abreast of developments by officers at parish level, while the whole structure was served by a dozen technical committees providing the advice necessary for effective implementation of policy.[7] (Plate 6)

The Warag was all-powerful with its intrusive tentacles touching many aspects of rural life. Beyond the administration of subsidies and agricultural credit facilities, the organisation of volunteer labour, the supervision of feed and fertiliser rationing schemes and the distribution of 'lease/lend' farm machinery, the Warag was involved in a plethora of other activities. Locally,

Plate 6. Farmers and War Agricultural Executive Committee members visiting a farm in Cardiganshire, 1942 (by permission of the National Library of Wales)

it coordinated materials recycling schemes managed by the Women's Voluntary Service, supervised the Women's Institute 'Dig for Victory' enterprises, arranged for Girl Guides and Boy Scouts to become involved with essential farm activities, and promoted rabbit and pest control. But these were minor issues compared with the Committees' central role in orchestrating and enforcing the government's plough-up policy, by which food production, and more especially the growing of wheat and potatoes, was given absolute priority.

As each county received its 'plough-up' quota, it was the duty of the county Warag, by offering advice, mounting demonstrations, providing machinery and other measures, to make sure that the quota was met. The Welsh county quotas, set at approximately half the acreage lost to the plough since 1918, are set out in Table 3.

Table 3. Wartime ploughing quotas and grassland ploughed in Wales (acres).[8]

County	Warag Quotas	Grassland ploughed (June 1939–May 1940)
Anglesey	10,000	11,000
Brecon	10,000	15,188
Cardigan	15,000	18,100
Carmarthen	30,000	35,261
Caernarvon	10,000	10,920
Denbigh	20,000	20,915
Flint	10,000	11,528
Glamorgan	15,000	17,454
Merioneth	5,000	6,026
Monmouth	15,000	16,060
Montgomery	15,000	22,500
Pembroke	20,000	21,571
Radnor	5,000	8,646

The ploughing grant and the steep increase in arable prices were potent stimuli to action, but it soon became obvious that many individual farmers would be unable to fulfil their quotas due to environmental or edaphic factors. In these cases prudent committees operated a policy of flexibility and compromise and exercised common sense in their dealings with farmers. Take, for example, the activities of the Llanfyllin District Committee of the Montgomeryshire Warag.[9] In what was predominantly a livestock rearing area, there seemed little sense in strictly applying wheat quotas. Accordingly the committee took the view that the £2 ploughing grant should be available to farmers growing turnips, rape and kale, while those farming less than 25 acres were excused from ploughing for cereals, provided they agreed to grow an acre or so of potatoes. By the same token, they listened carefully to the arguments of farmers who complained that illness had prevented them from meeting their quotas, or that their holdings lacked the facilities for threshing and storing grain. If common sense prevailed in Llanfyllin, it was not always so, with Warags in Cardiganshire and Carmarthenshire, in particular, being accused of enforcing impractical and inappropriate Cultivation Orders on increasingly embittered farmers.[10]

Irrespective of this, county Warags across the whole land of Wales strained every sinew to promote increased productivity. Ministers were excavated from their London offices and dragged off to draughty parish halls and windswept market squares in the far-flung reaches of west Wales where they exhorted farmers to ever-greater efforts. Technical experts from universities and colleges, seconded to the Warags for the duration, wrote advisory pamphlets, mounted demonstrations of improved farming methods and lectured on husbandry practices. (Plate 7) Farmers' wives and countrywomen of all ages and classes were instructed by stalwarts from the Women's Voluntary Service and the Women's Institute on such arcane procedures as jam making and skin curing and, for that matter, all aspects of 'make do and mend'. While the women stirred their preserving pans and their husbands worried over their Cultivation Orders, Warag propagandists placed dramatic half-page spreads in the local papers,[11] their patriotic jingles leaving little doubt as to the urgency of the job in hand:

Farmers! Plough by day and night. Play your part in the fight for right.

Ploughing on farms as vital as arms.

Win your Graf Spee battle of production by ploughing up now![12]

44

Plate 7. J. L. Johns, County Agricultural Education Organiser for Montgomeryshire conducting a 'fireside chat' with a group at Llangyniew (by permission of the National Library of Wales)

Of all the various Warag officers, the task of the Labour Officer was probably the most exacting. As farm workers left the land at the beginning of the war to seek more remunerative work building aerodromes or labouring in munitions factories, the County Labour Officer was charged with the awkward balancing act of ensuring that those eligible for military service duly took up arms, while concurrently securing sufficient labour for the land at vital times of the farming year. To this end, Labour Officers identified urban volunteers, conscientious objectors, retired workers and locally posted off-duty military personnel to lend a hand at haymaking and to help during the all–important cereal and potato harvests.

Efforts to persuade young Welsh women to join the Women's Land Army were of limited success, possibly because so many wives and daughters were already fully occupied on their home farms. However, a phalanx of girls from the industrial areas of

Lancashire and Cheshire readily joined the army and typically found their way to mid-Wales where the Breconshire and Radnorshire Women's Land Army secretariat arranged for them to be billeted in hostels in Brecon, Crossgates and Maesllwch Castle. From these centres they sallied out to long days of unremitting labour under the critical eye of the rural wiseacres who initially regarded them with suspicion and even contempt, but eventually came to appreciate their remarkable contribution to the war effort. By 1944, 2,427 members of the Women's Land Army worked on Welsh farms, the numbers gradually declining towards the end of the war as recruiting efforts began to slacken off.[13] By this time, in any case, growing numbers of prisoners-of-war were available following General Wavell's successes in North Africa where 117,000 Italian prisoners were taken. Following the armistice with Italy in 1943, 54,000 Italians were working on British farms, their numbers subsequently being reinforced by captured Germans.[14] Initially located in camps and later, in some cases, billeted on farms, almost 3,700 prisoners worked on the land in Wales, their organisation and disposition coming directly within the remit of the County Labour Officer. This influx equally applied to the East European and Baltic guest workers who came to work the land on fixed-term contracts in the early postwar years, a number of them lodged at a camp at Llannon in Cardiganshire. Anxious to reduce costs, the authorities tried to have them billeted on local farms. However, as John Lewis, Labour Officer for the area pointed out in his answer to a Ministry of Agriculture questionnaire, despite all his efforts to persuade them of the benefits of billeting, volunteers were chary of leaving the communal pleasures of the hostel. They could not, he noted, contemplate the loneliness of farm life and the inevitable language difficulties.[15]

As gardens and roadside verges were dug and playing fields cultivated, and as Irish labourers and prisoners-of-war reclaimed parts of Cors Fochno in Cardiganshire and struggled to grow potatoes at high elevations in Montgomeryshire, Warag officers turned to another source of labour, the nation's children. In a controversial policy move in the first year of the war, the government took action to engage schoolchildren in the food production campaign. Against the objections of the Trades Union Congress, and especially the teaching unions, school holidays were fixed to coincide with peak seasonal demand for farm work. Even more controversially, an arrangement was made whereby children could absent themselves from school in order to work on farms for up to 20 half days annually during term time. In parallel with these measures the Warags in Pembrokeshire, Caernarvonshire, Flint and Montgomeryshire organised fortnightly 'harvest camps' during which children helped with the corn and potato harvests. As a result, schoolchildren in Wales and England contributed a total of 268,860 and 274,752 boy/girl weeks of work in the peak years of 1942 and 1943, all undertaken under the watchful eye of volunteer teachers and Warag personnel.[16] (Plate 8)

Welsh school logbooks provide a vivid picture of these activities. In the Cardiganshire villages of Penrhyncoch and Eglwysfach,

Plate 8. Schoolboys harvesting potatoes (by permission of the Museum of English Rural Life, University of Reading)

schools were closed for a week in October to allow pupils to gather the potato harvest. Again, the headmaster of Brynherbert School, Llanrhystud in the same county reported annually that attendance was poor in the weeks leading up to Christmas as children were kept at home preparing poultry for the market. A few miles away, Tregaron School opened on 14 July 1941 after two weeks closure for the summer holiday. But many children stayed away due, as the headmaster declared in the logbook, to sheep shearing still being in progress, "… and several of the senior boys have not returned from the mountain".[17] This was only part of the story. During school hours children collected rose hips for conversion to Vitamin C for the forces, gathered sphagnum moss for incorporation into field dressings, picked blackberries for the Women's Institute's jam making enterprises, and foraged for all manner of medicinal plants including foxglove, coltsfoot, centaury and yarrow. It was in all an extraordinary effort, whose full details are yet to be recorded. (Plate 9)

Plate 9. "We're doing our bit"; crushing rosehips for the troops (by permission of the Museum of English Rural Life, University of Reading)

Ruthless Rascality: Grading Farms and Farmers

When the government introduced the National Farm Survey of 1941–3, the Warags embarked upon what was arguably the most controversial of their many roles. The survey took in all holdings of more than five acres, and had the primary purpose of evaluating the efficiency of individual farms so that underperformers could be identified and persuaded or compelled to improve their efforts.[18] It was a massive exercise in surveillance and scrutiny, requiring the attention of personnel who were both technically well-versed and also capable of fair and unbiased judgement in assessing the capabilities of farms and farmers. (Plate 10) The plan was to grade farms within the following categories:

A. Farms achieving 80 per cent or above of potential output.

B. Farms achieving between 60 and 80 per cent of potential output.

C. Farms achieving less than 60 per cent of potential output.

By way of the device of the Cultivation Order, a document specifying the acreage of crops to be grown on each farm and providing husbandry advice to be followed, the 'C' farm could be progressively upgraded.

Plate 10. Ridging potatoes near Erwood, Breconshire, c.1940

Among the many difficulties implicit in this approach was that of achieving consistency, in that cases could arise where a farm was rated 'C' in one district, whereas a comparable holding might be assessed 'B' in another district where standards were perhaps a little less rigorous. Inevitably, there were dark hints that personal animosities might come into play, resulting in an individual and his farm being downgraded by an ill-intentioned appraiser. Even where District Committees responsible for deciding on farm classifications comprised impeccably unbiased individuals, the very fact that they had been appointed by the county Warag left open the door to the suggestion, if nothing more, of jobbery, favouritism and nepotism.

How did Welsh farmers view the Warags and their officers, "… that regiment of officials who have been given temporary commission to run the country (which) will soon develop into a permanent army of occupation"?[19] The balance of evidence seems to indicate that attitudes varied between counties depending on the quality of personnel, the degree of flexibility in their approach and the preparedness of county branches of the National Farmers Union (NFU) to persuade their membership of the need for cooperation. In Anglesey, Caernarvon, Montgomeryshire and Pembrokeshire, for example, amiable relationships between the NFU and Warag offices ensured ready cooperation throughout the war. In stark contrast though, the Warags of Carmarthenshire and Cardiganshire enjoyed less than convivial relationships either with the NFU or the farming community at large. Their committees, it was claimed, were 'unrepresentative' and obsessively driven by targets. They were accused of imposing 'grossly excessive' ploughing quotas, of enforcing wholly inappropriate Cultivation Orders and of ignoring the advice of people with detailed local knowledge. They were castigated for victimising individuals who failed to carry out absurdly unrealistic Cultivation Orders which they deemed to be against the best interests of the land. When technical officers of the Warag sent out Cultivation Orders which were impossible to implement due to shortages of labour or equipment, resentment and animosity were the inevitable consequence.[20]

And this resentment ran particularly deep in Cardiganshire where many viewed the virtually unrestricted powers of the Warag with profound suspicion. Helpful though Cultivation Orders were supposed to be, their demands and the associated advice often failed to recognise peculiar local circumstances, and this, it was alleged, caused the land to deteriorate. It was also widely believed that a bottle of whiskey here or a £10 note there could be powerfully persuasive in causing blind eyes to be turned at appropriate moments, and even these desirable sweeteners were unnecessary where a man had family links to a Warag official.[21]

The ultimate sanction of the Warag was the dispossession of allegedly incompetent farmers under the Cultivation of Lands Order of 1939. In such cases holdings could be taken by the Committees for the duration of the war and five years afterwards and either managed by the Committee itself or let to some more able farmer. Dispossession was very much a last-ditch scenario since it would be the prelude to a mountain of paperwork. Nevertheless, some 677,000 acres of Wales and England were taken over by County Committees, the Welsh figures being given in Table 4.[22]

Table 4. Welsh property requisitions by the County War Agricultural Executive Committees; the situation in 1946 (numbers).

County	Holdings	Total acreage	With farmhouses occupied by late occupier	Occupied and managed by CWAEC	Let to tenants
Anglesey	5	448	3	1	1
Brecon	13	2,218	8	11	2
Caernarvon	6	992	2	4	2
Cardigan	35	2,752	5	29	6
Carmarthen	52	5,862	9	40	12
Flint	3	302	0	0	3
Glamorgan	8	1,014	2	6	2
Merioneth	6	1,013	1	3	3
Denbigh	16	1,886	4	5	11
Monmouth	29	2,269	12	12	17
Montgomery	17	2,210	0	4	13
Pembroke	31	3,218	7	8	16
Radnor	15	2,827	0	11	4
Wales	226	27,001	53	134	92

It has sometimes been claimed that some District Committees behaved in a manner at best heavy-handed and at worst unsympathetic and dictatorial. Yet, after more than 60 years of myth making, with Welsh Warags being periodically demonised as heartless apparatchiks bent on settling old scores, it is difficult to find instances where the limited numbers of dispossessed farmers were not at least in part the architects of their own misfortunes.

Irrespective of subversive mutterings in pubs, chapels and elsewhere, abuse of power seems to have been very rare. There may have been the occasional rotten apple in the barrel but, on balance, the Welsh evidence suggests that Warag officers at the District and Technical Committee level were carefully selected on the basis of their technical competence, diplomacy and common sense. Yet, when viewed in the context of an inward-looking and essentially conservative rural society, where everyone's business was common currency, it is hardly surprising that when a young graduate from beyond the community was thrust by the Warag into a position of local power, he became a target for gossip and calumny. However enthusiastic, able and fair-minded he might be, he could hardly avoid ruffling a few local feathers!

Given that Britain was engaged in total war against fascism, it seems a nice irony that the battle on the Home Front was conducted with a degree of quasi-fascist control which would have gladdened the heart of any corporate state theorist. But the battle was fought to good effect. Undemocratic and bureaucratically unwieldy they may have been, yet the Warags helped to forge a productive industry from one that had suffered from a generation of neglect. More food may have been grown in the absence of Warag controls, but whether it would have been the *right* food is quite another matter.[23] (Plate 11)

Plate 11. Captain and Mrs Bennett-Evans and their daughter stacking oats on a tripod on the slopes of Pumlumon, 1942 (by permission of the National Library of Wales)

A Changed Landscape

With the support and encouragement of the Warags, Welsh farmers transformed the face of Wales in the years after 1939. As land was absorbed for aerodromes and military training facilities (as with the 40,000 acres of the Mynydd Epynt in Breconshire), large-scale reclamation work was undertaken elsewhere. Lime and basic slag use on both hill and lowland increased sixfold between 1939 and 1945, and the cultivated area of Wales expanded by a half a million acres over the same period. The overall effects of the 'plough-up' campaign, in which the government sought, above all, to stimulate the growth of bulky crops for direct human consumption, are summarised in Table 5.[24]

Table 5. Temporal changes in acreage of crops and potatoes in Wales, 1940–5.

Year	Wheat	Barley	Oats	Potatoes
1940	31,500	34,200	284,600	36,900
1941	63,700	50,900	354,300	68,200
1942	82,500	62,900	403,300	81,800
1943	132,800	85,900	369,500	67,300
1944	113,000	80,400	347,800	67,100
1945	59,000	67,600	332,500	75,000

Throughout the whole of the war soil fertility was maintained by way of careful rotational practice, so that the Welsh acreage of turnips and swedes grown in rotation advanced by 75 per cent by 1945. Aided by practically-based advisory bulletins compiled by staff from the Universities at Aberystwyth and Bangor, farmers aimed as closely as possible to achieve on-farm self-sufficiency. The judicious use of scarce artificial fertilisers had had a role in the first years of the war, but the Phosphates Fertilisers Order of September 1942 prohibited the use of phosphates on grassland, thereby emphasising the importance of the retention and recycling of organic manures.[25] Two months later the Foodstuffs (Rationing) Order declared that henceforth off-farm animal feeds would only be available under a strictly controlled ration card system, which meant, in effect, that Welsh livestock farmers would have to produce ever more starches and proteins from their own resources.[26] This prompted a steep increase in the output of oats and pulses (especially for working horses of which there remained 97,000 in 1946), and of green crops for cattle and sheep. Meanwhile, the pre-war trend towards milk production continued, with the size of the dairy herd increasing by 18 per cent between 1939 and 1946, alongside an advance in total cattle numbers of almost 70,000. The sheep population, on the other hand, declined marginally from 2.4 million breeding ewes at the beginning of the war to 2.2 million by 1946. Consonant with the strict limitations on the availability of feedstuffs, breeding sow numbers collapsed to a mere 11,247 in the same year.

Like farmers elsewhere in Britain, Welsh farmers in general had a good war. There may have been little real progress in crop or livestock outputs on a per acre basis, yet advancing prices ensured that competent and efficient farmers in most sectors were able to profit. The availability of Exchequer aid for lime, slag, drainage and various infrastructural improvements rescued many farms from the decrepitude into which they had sunk for almost a generation. Equally important, public perception of the farmer had improved beyond measure. By helping to feed the nation and thereby freeing scarce resources for the production of tanks and guns, farmers in Wales and England had played a pivotal role in winning the war. Contemporary observers witnessed a sea change in attitudes towards the land and could see before them a countryside transformed and a farmscape devoted to maximising productivity. It may be impossible to gauge the psychological effect of this fillip to his status on the Welsh farmer in general. Yet, it is not difficult to imagine that as he went about his daily work he did so with growing confidence in the importance of his vocation. Proud of his achievements and warmed by public approval, he might dream of reaping his reward in a postwar era of expansion and prosperity, underpinned by seemingly inexorable scientific advances. For many Welsh farmers in the livestock sector, however, the idea of genuine and significant increases in prosperity would for some years remain little more than a pleasant dream.

CHAPTER THREE

Postwar Revolution

Moving Forward

ONCE THE WAR HAD come to an end there was a general consensus among politicians that the implementation of long-term strategies for agriculture would only be feasible with a high level of government intervention. With this in mind the postwar Labour Government retained an element of control over the countryside by way of the County Agricultural Executive Committees which coordinated Ministry of Agriculture policy at the local level.[1] Under the popular and highly effective minister, Tom Williams, farming was on the threshold of a period of rapid and sustained growth.[2] Indeed, agricultural output rose more rapidly between 1945 and 1965 than at any time before or since.[3] Labour's policies, leading to stable and rising prices underpinned by Exchequer subsidies, created a climate of growing confidence leading to an unprecedented uptake of new technology over the 20-year period.[4]

But progress was halting in the first few years. Postwar Britain was, after all, virtually bankrupt, and for many people the austerity and rationing of the late 1940s struck as deeply as in the war years themselves.[5] The discontinuation of 'lease/lend' in August 1945, the appalling winter of 1946–7 when over 4 million ewes died, and the balance of payments crisis of 1947, eventually culminated in the devaluation of the pound in 1949. Funds were rapidly running out and the government took the view that further balance of payments crises would only be avoided by massive increases in home production, and this applied especially to food. The creation of a stable and effective agricultural sector, with fair returns to farmers and land workers, was seen as a *sine qua non* of national reconstruction. (Plate 12)

The 1947 Agriculture Act, the keystone of legislation underpinning policy before Britain's entry into the European Community, was drafted specifically to meet this objective. Designed to convert wartime policies into a workable peacetime programme, it was essentially a farmers' act and contained virtually no provisions for addressing the social or economic problems of rural society. The Act identified the principles of good farming, established a land tribunal, encouraged the provision of council smallholdings, formalised the status of the County Agricultural Executive Committees and provided the framework for the

Plate 12. Postwar cultivation; Carmarthenshire, 1951

formation of the National Agricultural Advisory Service.[6] Above all, though, it introduced an era of guaranteed prices sustained, where necessary, by deficiency payments.[7]

The intentions of the Act were soon realised. In the certain knowledge that they were not to be abandoned to world market forces, as had been the case after 1921, farmers invested in buildings, machinery, drainage and other infrastructural improvements. With free advice from the newly-established National Agricultural Advisory Service readily to hand, they responded enthusiastically so that by the early 1950s, agricultural output exceeded the 1936–9 level by 20 per cent. The Conservatives returned to power in 1951 armed with a portfolio of policies aimed at advancing this figure to no less than 60 per cent. This would be achieved by the removal of remaining wartime restrictions on machinery purchase and, in particular, by stimulating beef and sheep production via the efficient use of grassland nourished by subsidised nitrogenous fertilisers. In addition, encouragement was given to the marketing boards, originally established in the 1930s, while a massive campaign was launched against the rabbit, that scourge of productive farming whose numbers would eventually be decimated in the myxomatosis pandemic of 1952–3.[8]

Yet there remained a conundrum. While increased output was essential as a means of protecting the precarious balance of payments situation, this could only be achieved at the cost of massive Exchequer support. Besides, taking advantage of the price system meant investing capital in plant and machinery, and more often than not, only the larger and more entrepreneurially-minded farmer had access to the required funds. Even a modest shift in practice, such as changing from hay to silage making, demanded not only a new knowledge base, but the investment of levels of capital often beyond the pocket of the smaller farmer.[9] Not surprisingly, this led to dissatisfaction, if not resentment, in some sectors of the industry and it was against this background that many Welsh farmers withdrew their support from the NFU in 1953 and formed their own organisation, the Farmers Union of Wales. (Plate 13)

Plate 13. Sheep shearing in Meirionethshire, 1951

Wales – Another Country

Whether or not a farmer could take full advantage of the opportunities offered by government guarantees and deficiency payments depended in large measure on his managerial ability, his aspirations and the location of his farm. Except for those on the lowland fringes, few farmers in Wales could benefit from the opportunities available to the large arable producer elsewhere in Britain. The Hill Farming Act of 1946, the first ever element of peacetime legislation for the hills and uplands, provided grants for farm improvement, and by 1949 there were 2,000 schemes in operation in Wales and England. But this Act and the 1951 Livestock Rearing Act (which extended the area available for grant and the total sum of money allotted) had relatively limited effects in Wales since, as the *Mid Wales Investigational Report* noted, many farmers were in too small a way of business to respond to their provisions.[10] Help was at hand in the form of the Small Farm Assistance Scheme (1958), although once again, apprehensive of the motives of the state and traditionally suspicious of state direction, many farmers chose not to take part.

Various official reports, including the 1953 White Paper, *Rural Wales* and the *Mid Wales Investigational Report* of two years later highlighted the importance of expanding the basic land-using industries in Wales and emphasised the economic and socio-cultural challenges of hill and upland areas. Depopulation remained a major problem and would continue to be so until employment opportunities, social amenities and public utilities were significantly improved. A steady falling away of the primary social population, it was believed, would lead not only to the eventual collapse of the hill livestock sector, (an essential link in the stratification of the lowland livestock industry), but to the withering away of an old way of life pivotal to the very fabric of Wales. (Plate 14)

Plate 14. The loss of an older way of life; the wheelwright's shop

Selective Expansion

It was all very well for academics and ruralists to lament the decay of the remote Welsh countryside, but by the mid-1950s, policy makers in Whitehall were becoming alarmed by the escalating cost of agricultural support. The 1957 Agriculture Act recognised this by introducing the principle of selective expansion. The idea here was to direct production grants and other forms of Exchequer assistance away from the expansion of output at all costs and towards a wholesale improvement in agricultural *efficiency*. (Plate 15) This implied careful targeting of aid with respect both to specific enterprises and to the managerial capacities of individual farmers. There was, moreover, a general presumption that efficiencies would be affected if unit sizes increased and various pieces of enabling legislation in the 1960s offered incentives for farm amalgamation and farmer retirement. These were of little significance in Wales. Relatively hard-up and capital-starved they may have been, yet few smaller farmers were ready to surrender their way of life, their sturdy independence, their birth right even, for some sort of government pension. The older among them preferred the old home, the old ways and the old associations. (Plate 16)

If there remained financial hardship in the hills and uplands and among many smaller farmers, Welsh farming, on the whole, shared in the two decades of growth between the end of the war and the mid-1960s. As the arable area declined from its wartime peak, ever-growing emphasis was placed on livestock production. Even the breeding sow population recovered to its pre-war level.[11] Renovation of grassland, leading to a reduction of more than 200,000 acres of rough grazing, was paralleled by a 45 per cent increase in the size of the breeding ewe flock, while the dairy sector forged ahead with a threefold expansion in the number of cows and

Plate 15. Innovation in forage conservation; T. L. Phillips of Llanboidy, Carmarthenshire admires his brick-built circular silo

Plate 16. Wartime cultivations in Montgomeryshire; Mr Price of Aberbechan, Newtown

heifers in milk between 1946 and 1966. By the mid-1960s, the Milk Marketing Board was purchasing more than 280 million gallons annually from some 40,000 registered milk producers.[12] Virtually all cows were now milked by machine, while dairymen enthused over the potential for artificial insemination and readily adopted new veterinary and pharmaceutical approaches for the control of mastitis, milk fever and other bovine conditions. With efficient milk production from grass being the primary focus of government policy (enthusiastically propagandised by advisors from the National Agricultural Advisory Service and the Welsh Plant Breeding Station), large acreages were drained and limed and stocking densities subsequently improved through the use of cheap nitrogenous fertiliser. Integral to grassland management were hay and silage-making and as these tasks became more technically sophisticated, so did the mechanisation of the Welsh farm forge ahead. By 1966 there were no less than 44,000 tractors in Wales along with 12,000 balers, 16,000 muck spreaders and 28,000 mowing machines. (Plate 17)

And, as these machines arrived at the farm gate, they bade farewell to hired labourers as they walked out. At the close of the war, more than 52,000 farm workers supported the industry; a mere 28,000 remained 20 years later. The cultural implications of this haemorrhage provoked concern in some quarters, but most people viewed the substitution of machinery for labour as a rational procedure, a sensible move at a time when economic efficiency took precedence over other considerations.

A Little too Far Perhaps?

For more than a quarter of a century after the war, the agricultural policies of successive British governments had been devoted to maintaining farm incomes and promoting efficiency across the diverse sectors of the industry. Concurrently, the expanding wealth of consumers had stimulated demand for both traditional

Plate 17. The 'little grey Fergie', helpmate of many a farmer in Wales in the early postwar decades

and luxury agricultural products and creative links had been forged between the farming industry and the wholesale/retail sectors. But for all the apparent dynamism of the farming world, the cost of sustaining it continued to bear heavily upon the Exchequer by the early 1970s. Moreover, it was becoming only too obvious that a disproportionate amount of support was finding its way into the pockets of the larger farmers. Thus, was the much maligned culture of 'agribusiness' being underwritten by a progressively more restive taxpaying public, who were beginning to resent the advance of agricultural intensification? Hundreds of miles of hedgerows had been removed to accommodate larger machinery, ponds had been filled in, woodlands grubbed out and traditional farm buildings replaced with quasi-industrial structures.

In academic common rooms and around urban dining tables questions began to be asked (often in an atmosphere of alarming ignorance), about the moral and ethical aspects of intensive livestock production. At the same time, the urban intelligentsia began to attack the widespread and sometimes excessive use of agrochemicals and to query the overall effects of modern farming on the quality and diversity of the natural environment. If more heat than light was generated as the arguments were played out in the press and the broadcast media, the simple fact was that the taxpayer was no longer prepared to give unquestioning support to an industry which it perceived to be abandoning its traditional role as conservator of the countryside. (Plate 18) Anyhow, the argument went, why should the taxpayer support an economic sector which by now was producing surplus output, much of it unceremoniously dumped on the world market?

So it was that when Britain entered the European Common Market in 1973, much of the burden of agricultural support was transferred, by way of the Common Agricultural Policy, from the taxpayer to the consumer. Predictably, food prices rose steeply as Britain surrendered her economic independence. Henceforth, the financial fortunes of farming, the cost of food to the consumer and the maintenance of the landscape in Wales and England would be dictated in large measure by notions originating in Brussels.

Plate 18. Postwar grassland management: spreading lime by hand, Llyfnant valley, 1952

Less Favoured Areas

The various initiatives of the 1950s, '60s and early '70s had helped many farmers to improve the physical layout of their buildings and to drain and reclaim significant acreages of unproductive land in Wales. But the perennial problem of the hills and uplands still remained. People were still leaving the land. The average age of farmers was drifting ever upwards and traditional trades and industries continued to wane.[13] In an attempt to create a body capable of strengthening the economic fabric of these beautiful, yet steadily declining parts of the country, the Welsh Office set up the Development Board for Rural Wales in 1977. The board, it was fondly hoped, would be the principal instrument of economic activity as it awarded grants to stimulate diversification and tourism and to encourage farm pluriactivity. The board may have achieved some success in encouraging industrial development as an element in the expansion of Newtown in Powys, but its influence on the farming world was less impressive. After all, to foster change among a hill farming population which, for generations, had prided itself on producing food for the nation was, in itself, a challenging prospect. Diversification involved major cultural and attitudinal changes while pluriactivity was only really feasible in situations where surplus family labour could be absorbed within the framework of local employment. The Board's problems were intensified by the difficulties of the prevailing economic climate. The imposition of strict quotas on dairy farms in 1984 and concurrent restrictions on the eligibility for subsidy on sheep and breeding cows were savage blows to the prosperity of many, coming as they did at a time of rising interest rates.

The European Union's 'Less Favoured Areas Scheme', initiated in the 1980s, was to become the principal instrument of agricultural support for much of Wales. The scheme, aimed at maintaining the integrity of fragile social and economic structures in rural areas, embraced three quarters of the agricultural acreage of the country and almost 70 per cent of her farms. A major element involved the introduction of the so-called 'Hill Livestock Compensatory Allowances', by which support was given to farmers in the form of headage payments for beef cattle and sheep. The environmental effects on the 250,000 acres of semi-natural grassland reclaimed between 1966 and 1986 were only too predictable. As sheep numbers expanded relative to those of cattle, with sheep densities reaching four times those of the 1950s, overgrazing and environmental destabilisation occurred. This was not, of course, universally the case. The relationship between stocking density and vegetation change is complex and variable, so that the same level of stocking density might give rise to serious levels of ecological damage in one place and relatively little elsewhere. On the whole, though, the headage payment arrangements were perceived to have had an adverse affect upon a range of wildlife habitats.[14] But, irrespective of the criticism levelled at headage payments, they were by no means entirely the villain of the piece. Given that there was a marginal increase in the total labour force on Welsh farms between 1986 and 1999 (where farmers, partners and directors are included), it could be claimed that the support system had helped, at least in part, to stem population decline.[15]

A Beleaguered Industry

Throughout the 1980s and 1990s public pressure, fuelled by increasingly frenzied media outbursts, persuaded the official world to turn its attention away from maintaining modern agricultural productivity, towards a greener agenda embracing environmental protection and sustainable (if not organic) farming methods. To many working farmers, indeed, the passing of the Wildlife and Countryside Act of 1981 seemed to signify the apparent abandonment of any serious interest in food production in favour of the protection of wildlife habitats. The public as a whole, however, saw the Act as a perfectly reasonable reaction to the perceived environmental damage wrought by the intensification of the previous three decades. The worst excesses may have been committed in the east of England, but there was a widely held view that all farmers, irrespective of their acreage or location, were, so to speak, 'tarred with the same brush'. Quangos, meanwhile, which seemed to thrive like thistles, vied with each other to launch landscape and wildlife conservation initiatives. Costly academic studies and the reports of focus group musings stressed, time and again, the importance attached by the public not only to environmental protection, but also to the actual sources of the food they consumed. Farmers read of these works with a growing sense of isolation and frustration and, as they did so, they pondered upon the antics of the Animal Liberation Front, the hunt saboteurs and the campaigners against the transport of live animals. Their vocation, it appeared, was under threat and their industry under siege.

The farming industry, of course, is a broad church. Arable producers prospered with the fall in the value of the pound subsequent to Britain's withdrawal from the European Exchange Rate Mechanism in September 1992, while increases in the value of land strengthened the capital base of farmers in the more favourable lowlands. On the whole, livestock producers in the uplands and milk producers elsewhere did not share their good fortune and were confronted by rising costs and falling prices in the closing years of the twentieth century.

The economic problems of the Welsh livestock industry, already suffering from the after-effects of the Chernobyl nuclear disaster of 1986, were compounded ten years later by the catastrophic outbreak of Bovine Spongiform Encephalopathy (BSE) which prompted the prohibition of beef exports to Europe for a two-year period. As pestilence stalked the land (to return again in the form of Foot and Mouth Disease in 2001), and herds and flocks were decimated, the leaden hand of bureaucracy tightened its baleful grip. Farmers, especially the older ones, felt they were caught up in an unequal struggle with an uncaring urban world and a political class which had somehow abandoned any idea of fostering a productive and dynamic countryside. As commentators and pundits blamed the greed and avarice of the livestock industry for the miseries of Foot and Mouth Disease and its devastating effects on the tourist industry, its practitioners dug in and awaited the next disaster.[16]

A New Way Forward?

While livestock farmers in Wales contemplated an uncertain future, the view continued to prevail in the councils of Europe that communities in remote areas remained worthy of protection. The European Union Agri-Environmental Regulation of 1992 had introduced the concept of Environmentally Sensitive Areas, wherein farmers received direct payments for pursuing husbandry systems which met specific conservation objectives.[17] Within, and eventually beyond, the six Welsh Environmentally Sensitive Areas, the Habitat Scheme and its successors, *Tir Cymen*, *Tir Gofal* and *Tir Cynnal*, sought to replace production-based support with payments to promote a framework of land management in the interests of society as a whole. Subsequent changes to the framework of the Common Agricultural Policy in 2003 ushered in the notion of the Single Payment Scheme and the principles of cross compliance, embodying a holistic approach to environmental standards, food supply and animal health and welfare. Henceforth agricultural activity throughout much of Wales would be an essential, if not the primary element within a pattern of policies focussed on maintaining the natural environment and supporting tourism.

Since the late 1960s a modest group of pioneers in Wales had been quietly resurrecting the ideas of organic farming promulgated by Lady Eve Balfour, Rolf Gardiner and others during the interwar years.[18] With increasing public concern over the excessive use of agro-chemicals and worries about the alleged damage to the environment brought about by modern farming methods, the demand for organically-produced foods began to grow rapidly. Prompted by support from the Welsh Assembly Government and the Organic Centre Wales, established at Aberystwyth in 2000, a growing number of farmers set upon the path of conversion to organic methods. For a while, aggressive and sophisticated marketing, together with well-directed media presentation, ensured buoyancy of demand for Welsh organic produce. The proportion of agricultural land managed organically increased at an annual rate of more than 20 per cent between 2006 and 2008, as more farmers entered conversion arrangements. The number of organically reared beef cows and ewes expanded by 35 and 47 per cent respectively over the same period and by 2008, some 8 per cent of Wales was under organic production.[19] At the time of writing, national and local economic circumstances seem temporarily to have nipped this development in the bud. However, in view of the strong commitment to organic farming by the Welsh Assembly Government, the general enthusiasm for organic food and the pan-European demand both for conventionally and organically produced Welsh lamb, there is every possibility that the sector will recover as the present recession becomes a memory.

The Path Ahead

Despite the shocks and traumas of the past 20 years, visitors to rural Wales still find themselves in an essentially agricultural landscape. If the twin hammers of bureaucracy and animal health legislation have crushed pig production in Wales, livestock continue to represent 71 per cent of the gross output of Welsh farms. Dairy herd numbers have steadily contracted, yet there remain over 280,000 cows in the country with average number of cows per herd having moved from 53 to 83 over the past ten years. In the same period, beef cow numbers have advanced by 50,000 and the total number of sheep in the country stands in excess of nine millions. Cereals, potatoes and market garden crops continue to be grown in those areas which supported them a century or more ago and the great stone walls of the north and hedge banks of the south still remain much as they were in 1936. Houses and buildings may have changed, signs advertising the blandishments of bed and breakfast, pony trekking, paintballing and kindred diversions may have mushroomed, but the land stays on. The pattern of farming past and present remains for all who have an eye to see it.

But, the future is far from certain. The contribution of agriculture to Welsh gross domestic product is likely to remain modest, yet it would be the height of folly for legislators to heed the advice of those who propose the virtual abandonment of farming in the less favoured areas, if not elsewhere. Such a move would launch an avalanche of environmental, social and cultural devastation, to say nothing of the negative effects upon tourism. Those who favour such apocalyptic notions would do well to note the results of surveys of visitors to Wales which invariably underline the absolute importance of a well-farmed landscape to overall visitor satisfaction.[20] In this context it is worth remembering that attempts at fostering 'off-farm' activities as a means of boosting farm incomes should always have regard for the integrity of the farmstead and landscape. (Plate 19) The Welsh countryside, after all, is a fragile creature which has for centuries been moulded and nurtured by farmers and their families. Its unique beauties will only be retained if the farming population and those of the rural community, who rely upon it, are allowed to fulfil their age-old function. Well-farmed land, husbanded by men and women sensitive to the ecological requirements of the natural world, will eventually yield the rich and diverse

Plate 19. Farming and tourism: Gwyn and Gareth Jones, Morfa, Llanrhystud, work against a background of caravans, 2011

environment which the tourist and urban taxpayer have come to demand.

There is, of course, every justification for arguing that since up to 40 per cent of the incomes of Welsh farmers derive from some form of subsidy, the tax paying paymaster should have some say about how they go about their business. But ultimately, Welsh farmers want to *farm*. This being so, legislators and policy makers have a sacred obligation to avoid creating the sort of bureaucratic and economic straightjackets which detract from the farmer's capacity to do his or her duty by the land and by the public. The poignant words of Oliver Goldsmith retain the same resonance in the early twenty-first century as they had nearly two and a half centuries ago:

> *Ill fares the land, to hastening ills a prey,*
> *Where wealth accumulates and men decay;*
> *Princes and lords may flourish or may fade;*
> *A breath can make them as a breath has made;*
> *But a bold peasantry, their country's pride,*
> *When once destroyed, can never be supplied.*[21]

CHAPTER FOUR

The Origins of the Farm Business Survey

Victorian Prelude

BY THE FINAL QUARTER of the nineteenth century British agriculture was approaching the peak of a long period of expanding prosperity. The gloomy prognostications of the opponents of free trade had not come to pass and the repeal of the Corn Laws in the 1840s had had little adverse effect on the advance of farming fortunes. Leading farmers and landowners in Britain had readily taken on board the opportunities offered by developments in agricultural chemistry and engineering and, as the perceived benefits of new technologies became clear to those further down the farming ladder, the productivity of farming forged ahead. By 1880, indeed, before the grim realities of the Great Depression began seriously to be felt, British agriculture was the pride of its practitioners and the envy of the world.[1]

Many of these practitioners had learned their trade under their fathers' direction. Traditionally, the farming world had taken little interest in the writings of agricultural theorists and the more reactionary of its members scorned the prospect of 'book learning'. But, by the second half of the nineteenth century, an authoritative body of periodical agricultural literature began to appear, and found an eager readership among the more thoughtful and innovative farmers. In weekly and monthly journals, they read of studies of novel farming methods, of the benefits of mechanisation, of drainage, of the use of artificial fertilisers and of a bewildering range of inventions and developments almost beyond the imagination of their grandparents' generation.[2] They read too, of trends in markets and prices both at home and abroad and of the inestimable benefits of free trade to Britain and her expanding empire. In the years immediately before the flood of transatlantic and antipodean imports shattered the illusion, many of the more enterprising farmers felt themselves to be on the crest of a seemingly endless wave of prosperity.[3]

It was claimed in the early 1930s that many Welsh farmers could not keep abreast of these developments due to a shortage of published information in the local language. There were, it was averred, a mere four accessible agricultural texts in the Welsh language.[4] Indeed, when the academic and civil servant Cadwaladr Bryner Jones (1872–1954), published *Egwyddorion Gwrteithio* in the early twentieth century, he noted that in attempting to set out the scientific principles of manuring in Welsh, he was responding to the complaints of farmers that no reliable source of information on this subject was available in that tongue.[5] A number of short-lived journals offering comment on agricultural and rural matters had briefly flourished in the 1840s and 1850s, while later in the century *Baner ac Amserau Cymru* joined *Y Genedl Gymreig* as the most widely read newspaper among Welsh farming folk. But these papers devoted only a limited amount of space to practical farming matters and their agrarian content was essentially political, with a strong commitment to promoting the interests of farmers in the land debate and the vexed issue of the tithe. Besides, as Ieuan Gwynedd Jones noted, with respect to political comment in these and similar publications, the tortuous use of language

and circumlocution of argument tended to militate against
clarity and to blur the edges of reality.[6] How far the lack of
technical and scientific texts in the language spoken by the
majority of farmers provided a stumbling block to agricultural
progress in Wales in the later nineteenth and early twentieth
centuries remains a debatable question.[7]

Keeping Track

In common with farmers elsewhere, Welshmen regularly
noted down features of the weather and the seasons in their
diaries and notebooks. (Plate 20) They also recorded sales of
grain and livestock, purchases of equipment, labour payments,
building costs and myriad details of their busy daily lives. Few
individuals, though, kept the sort of records whereby they
could derive some idea of profit or loss via a simple account
and balance sheet, and the great majority had little idea of the
strengths and weaknesses of their businesses.[8] Some, perhaps,
had a vague notion of the direct costs of the major enterprises,
but such primitive accounting systems as were available
at the time tended to ignore them.[9] In this respect, Britain
lagged behind her competitors in Germany, Denmark and
the United States where systems of record keeping and farm
accounting had become well-established by the closing years
of the nineteenth century. In these countries, studies of the
political economy of agriculture, along with the evolution of
analytical and survey methods, had allowed for the dissection
of businesses and enterprises, so that meaningful economic and
financial advice could be offered to farmers and landowners.
In Britain, though, reliable farm costings were few and far
between by 1900, and the professional agricultural economist
wholly unknown.[10]

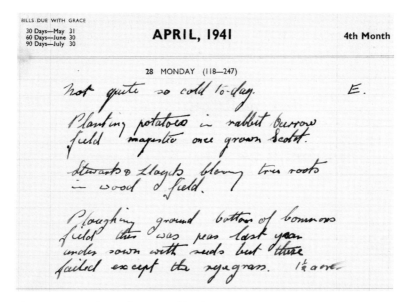

Plate 20. Extract from a farm record book

Wariness and Suspicion

In the two decades before the Great War and subsequently in the sporadically depressed years between the wars, distrust of government and suspicion of college-educated folk and so-called experts was almost endemic in the farming world. This was hardly surprising. Expert opinion had encouraged them to expand and develop their businesses, yet government, enslaved by the notion of free trade, had failed to come to their help in the 1890s and had let them down by abandoning wartime subsidies in 1921. Following the repeal of protectionist legislation that year, the great majority of farmers conceived a deep and long-term distrust of government agencies, however benign they may have seemed.[11] Smaller farmers in particular, and it has to be remembered that some three quarters of farms in 1925 were less than a 100 acres in size, would have little truck with the men from the Ministry and their appeals for innovation and forward thinking. After all, as far as they were concerned, government and officialdom had been responsible for the economic and financial mess against which they struggled to run their capital-starved enterprises and to avoid bankruptcy. They might have been responsive to technical advice, but they were wary of any attempt, however well meaning, to influence the economics of their holdings. Consequently they were normally unwilling to have their farms and any accounts they may have kept subject to external scrutiny. In effect, the antipathy and indifference of the majority to economic advice was not wholly wilful, but conditioned by the severe financial constraints under which they worked.

The Need for Change

By the outbreak of the Great War, change was in the air. As older farmers (often with some misgivings), grudgingly accepted the inevitable encroachment of science upon their craft, the more prosperous began to send their sons to one or other of the county or national agricultural colleges, established in the second half of the nineteenth century. Or, indeed, they may have enrolled them on courses offered by the various university departments opened in the 1880s and 1890s, whose activities were subject to the scrutiny and control of the Board, and subsequently Ministry of Agriculture. Their fathers may have distrusted 'book learning' yet many yielded to the idea that college training might just offer an opportunity for their sons to discover a new, exciting and profitable world.

The problem was that although these institutions offered a modicum of technical instruction they by and large avoided coverage of the financial and economic side of the farming industry. For generations agriculture had been seen as a creature wholly different in its structure and capital profile to urban industry, while farmers themselves were believed to be motivated by factors other than the mere pursuit of profit. Held to be a 'way of life', and an agreeable one at that, many people believed that farming could not, or should not, be subject to the same harsh mercantile realities as industry. But this view would soon change.

> The farmer's attention is frequently directed to the conduct of mercantile men who keep the most correct set of books, as an example to himself, but the admonition is given by men who do not understand the occupation of the farmer… The common sense view of the whole matter is this: Let the farmer keep only such books as he really requires to acquaint him with the state of his affairs.
>
> Henry Stephens, *The Book of the Farm* (Edinburgh, 1851).

As the virtual inevitability of war became accepted in the months leading up to August 1914, the official world pondered the potential effects of German submarine activity in the Atlantic.[12] It took no more than a moment's thought to conclude that if war broke out, transatlantic trade routes would become endangered and food supplies put at serious risk. In this case, farming would play a pivotal role in sustaining home food consumption, to say nothing of morale. Suddenly, an economy which had been almost totally ignored for a generation came increasingly into focus and people began at last to look upon British agriculture as an 'industry'.[13] The Ministry of Agriculture, long the Cinderella of government departments, grew steadily in prominence as did the views of agricultural strategists and thinkers. Men like the arch moderniser, Sir Daniel Hall (Plate 21) and the economist and historian, C.S Orwin, believed that the farming industry needed to be rationalised along the sort of lines that had transformed the manufacturing sector. If this was to occur, it was essential to accumulate a body of fundamental scientific data which would allow technological developments to proceed free of the empiricism and guesswork of the past. It was due in large measure to Hall's persistent lobbying that, in 1913, the Liberal government's Development Commission identified a number of institutions to which it would provide grant aid for specific areas of agricultural research. Among these were the John Innes Institute (plant breeding), Rothamsted (plant nutrition and soils), the Long Ashton Institute (fruit growing), Reading University (dairying) and Oxford University (agricultural economics).[14]

A New Discipline

The establishment of the Agricultural Economics Research Institute at Oxford provided *de facto* recognition of the compelling importance of streamlining and reconstructing a moribund economic sector. Only by a programme of reconstruction, it was widely believed, would farming be enabled to rise to the challenges of a tough future and to operate at acceptable levels of economic efficiency.

The first Director of the Institute, C.S. Orwin, (Plate 22) had taught at Wye College and served as agent for the Turnor estates in Lincolnshire before being appointed to the Oxford post which he held along with a fellowship at Balliol College. Like Sir Daniel Hall, Orwin was first and foremost a progressive. He argued for agricultural reconstruction, for the application of science and mechanisation to farming and for the expansion of unit sizes to exploit economies of scale.[15] Farmers, Orwin believed, were entrepreneurially sluggish and obscurantist, and he held firmly to the view that, irrespective of social consequences (notably the loss of the small, independent farmer), the future lay in full scale 'factory' farming along strictly scientific lines. Only the state, he argued, could reform the illogical and inefficient boundaries of farms and estates thereby creating the sort of large holdings which would attract graduates as tenants. Educated men alone, he stridently observed, should be allowed to farm the nation's land, and then only under the supervision of efficiency-minded land agents and county committees.[16]

Plate 21. Sir (Alfred) Daniel Hall, 1864–1942 (© Rothamsted Research Ltd)

Plate 22. Charles Stewart Orwin, 1876–1955 (© National Portrait Gallery, London)

It was clear to Orwin and his colleagues that this vision of an efficient, technologically-sophisticated farming sector located within a planned countryside would only ever be realised in the context of detailed knowledge of the physical and financial makeup of the industry. Hitherto, a mere handful of economists and political scientists had assembled piecemeal data on farming costs and returns. Yet no serious attempt had been made to organise the collection of information in such a way as to provide a scenario for financial help to farmers or strategic advice to government. An opportunity to address the problem presented itself with the repeal, in 1921, of the wartime Corn Production Act. In removing guaranteed prices from a range of products, repeal left the farming world exposed to the full effects of world prices and caused widespread consternation and despair throughout the sector. At the time Sir Daniel Hall was Permanent Secretary at the Ministry of Agriculture and he managed to provide some sweetening of what was an extremely bitter pill, by weaving into the Act of repeal the provision of £1 million to be specifically devoted to agricultural education and research. The money was eventually directed towards the establishment of Provincial Agricultural Advisory Centres at a number of universities and colleges in Wales and England. Quick to seize upon what seemed a golden opportunity, Orwin insisted that economists be included among the various specialists located at these centres and, in so doing, he laid the basis for the development of the profession of agricultural economics in Britain. By 1923, 'Advisory Economists' had been appointed at Wye College and at Reading and Cambridge Universities, to be followed shortly afterwards by similar appointments at the universities of Aberystwyth, Bristol, Newcastle and Manchester and at three agricultural colleges: Sutton Bonington in Nottinghamshire, Harper Adams in Shropshire and Seale-Hayne in Devon. These centres would become the focal points for vital studies of the structure and function of local agriculture and, in some cases, for the development of both fundamental and applied research in agricultural economics and rural sociology.

A New Man in Wales

It was to the provincial centre based at the University in Aberystwyth that Arthur W. Ashby (1886–1953) was appointed Advisory Economist in 1923. (Plate 23) Having left school at the age of twelve, Ashby had worked closely with his father, a well-respected small farmer and Liberal party activist living at Tysoe in Warwickshire.[17] After Ruskin College, Oxford, where he gained a diploma in economics and political science, Ashby worked briefly as political agent for the Liberal party, although he was eventually to become a staunchly loyal Labour supporter. Shortly after the election of 1910, he left for the University of Wisconsin to study agricultural economics, a well-established academic disciple in this, as in many American Land Grant colleges. He returned to work with Orwin at Oxford, concurrently serving as statistical assistant to the Agricultural Wages Board of which Orwin was a prominent member. A shy and rather diffident man, Ashby held powerfully strong social and political convictions, linked to a deep awareness of the vital importance of rebuilding the neglected economy of rural Britain. He believed profoundly in the fundamental need to maintain the economic and social cohesion of rural society, the achievement of which would require an understanding of the complex tensions, cultural networks and human associations making up the fabric of that society. Only by painstaking research, he believed, would it be possible properly to understand the nature of the present rural world and to make predictions about its future.

Creative, open-minded and extraordinarily energetic, Ashby was first and foremost an applied economist whose sympathy with the prevailing plight of the small Welsh farmer earned

Plate 23. Arthur W. Ashby, Professor of Agricultural Economics, 1929–46

him widespread popularity and respect. Meanwhile, a steady flow of research publications, often in collaboration with one or more of a close group of colleagues, would ensure that, in due course, Aberystwyth would become pre-eminent in the field of agricultural economics.[18]

Although not a Welsh speaker, Ashby laboured hard to understand the nature of the Welsh farmer and Welsh rural society. Within three years of his appointment he had established links with a variety of countryside organisations and, with the assistance of a group of cooperating farmers, had begun to investigate complex local economic problems. Never restricted in his approach by academic inhibitions, and equally at home with the farm worker as with the student in the lecture room, Ashby became an altogether pervasive presence in rural Wales between the time of his appointment in 1923 until his move to the directorship of the Oxford Institute following the retirement of Orwin in 1945. In the words of Thomas Lewis, a former colleague, Ashby looked at the Welsh countryside: "… as a priest looks at his parish, and nothing that happened in it was outside his active interest".[19]

Senseless Snobbery

However much he may have felt drawn to the more intellectually satisfying aspects of rural sociology and of the structure and function of the rural economy, Ashby never forgot that the primary purpose of the Provincial Advisory Centres was to collect physical and financial data. The Centres had been charged with assembling quantitative information which would not only form the basis for providing advice to farmers and rural organisations, but would establish some sort of rationale for official decision making. Furthermore, statistical material assembled and analysed by the Provincial Centres would serve to focus the minds of government, trades unions and farmers' representatives as they met to discuss the Annual Price Review, a pivotal event in the farming year from the time of the Second World War into the 1970s. Above all else, the Centres were expected to be wholly independent and objective in their methods.[20]

But herein lay a conundrum. The arrangements by which the Ministry of Agriculture provided grants to cooperating universities and colleges decreed that up to fifty per cent of the resources involved could be used for teaching and research, the remainder being devoted to data collection. This raised the predictable issue of divided loyalties and there remained for many years an uneasy and sometimes problematic relationship between the Advisory Economists and the academic institutions housing them. This apart, Ashby and his colleagues operated within a miasma of academic snobbery. Many of the Aberystwyth agricultural scientists, most of them from backgrounds in the pure sciences, viewed the agricultural economists, with their degrees in agriculture and interests in the practical realities of farming, with a sort of amused contempt. After all, men who daily set out via the local railway, bicycle or even horseback to meet working farmers, were surely quite beyond the academic pale! Try as they might, neither the agricultural scientists nor the other men of science in the University could bring themselves to see the agricultural economists as 'proper' academics, regarding them as a rather despised hybrid, in effect neither fish nor fowl.[21] If this struck in the collective craw of Ashby's men, the equally contemptuous attitude of the pure economists merely added to their sense of isolation.

Perhaps those who sneered at Ashby's attempts to establish agricultural economics as a respectable academic discipline had forgotten that the subject had been taught at Aberystwyth some years previously. As early as 1899, Edward Edwards of the Department of Economics and Political Science had delivered lectures in agricultural economics as a specialist course, while the subject was further developed by the economist, palaeographer and historian E.A. Lewis, head of the former Department between 1912 and 1931. In 1918 moreover, when the Development Commission rather worryingly suggested that the study of agriculture itself might seem more relevant to the practising farmer if approached from the standpoint of history and economics rather than being viewed essentially as an applied science, Lewis established a full course in agricultural economics for Aberystwyth students. Nonetheless, the economists remained sceptical, and many of the scientists looked upon their 'costings' colleagues with ill-concealed condescension. The latter, convinced of the value of their work, gritted their teeth and carried on, choosing to ignore the carping absurdities of their detractors.

New Men and a New Building

The fact that a number of the young men appointed to the fledgling Department of Agricultural Economics in the 1920s went on to play significant roles in Welsh rural life testifies both to their considerable abilities and their commitment to the cause. As funding from the Ministry of Agriculture steadily increased from £1,262 in 1924 to £2,620 in 1932, and the Welsh Agricultural Organisation Society contributed monies to support studies of agricultural marketing, Ashby was enabled to gradually expand his staffing complement. J. Pryse Howell was recruited from Oxford to take up the post of Assistant Advisor in 1925 and in the same year J. Morgan Jones and Tom Lewis were appointed as marketing assistants, being replaced by J. Llefelys Davies and T. Llewelyn Morgan in 1930. They were joined by W.H. Jones and E. Llewelyn Parry in 1932 and 1934 respectively.[22]

Like other universities and colleges, Aberystwyth was only too happy to accept grant aid from the Ministry of Agriculture and yet, at the same time, to locate its Provisional Advisory Centres in overcrowded and inadequate accommodation. Packed into a small corner of the Agricultural Buildings, themselves little more than an adapted iron foundry adjacent to Aberystwyth railway station, Ashby and his eight staff and three clerical assistants stoically stuck to their respective tasks. Surrounded by relics of the old iron works and the stains of sulphurous fumes, they perched on their second-hand stools and got down to the job as best they could. Appreciating fully the effects of working environment on morale, Ashby had for years lobbied the University authorities for decent accommodation. But it was only in 1937, almost a decade after Ashby had been appointed to the first Chair in Agricultural Economics in Britain, that the issue was addressed.

The first stage of Sir Percy Thomas's grand (and unhappily never fully realised) design for the vacant Penglais site had come into fruition with the completion of the structure eventually to become known as the Cledwyn Building.[23] (Plate 24) With its facing of Forest of Dean stone and its Pembrokeshire slate roof, the new building was a thing of dignity and elegance located in a situation of great natural beauty. Built with the aid of a £15,000

Treasury grant, match-funded by the University, this edifice would house the Welsh Plant Breeding Station, the Imperial Bureau of Plant Genetics (Herbage Plants) and the Department of Agricultural Economics. But grand and eloquent structures did not impress everyone. One notable critic of Thomas's plans was R.G. Stapledon who believed that university departments needed workshops rather than showcase buildings, "Whatever happens", he wrote sniffily to Principal Ivor Evans in the winter of 1934, "the Plant Breeding Station will never do better work than it has done in its cramped and inadequate quarters. And herein lies a general truth, the lesson of which it is difficult to translate."[24] Nevertheless Ashby was delighted. A new building, the availability of improved analytical equipment and an overall easing of the financial torpor of the previous few years had between them suggested every reason for optimism about the future.[25] Basic research would now proceed hand-in-hand with data gathering and, as more farmers perceived the value of the exercise, the more sophisticated and valuable the data would become.

Plate 24. The new agricultural building on the Penglais site

Out on the Road

For more than a decade Ashby, J. Pryse Howell, J. Morgan Jones and other colleagues had been encouraging Welsh farmers not only to keep records, but to make them available for external scrutiny. This in itself was no mean feat, and it is a remarkable testament to the personalities and sheer persistence of these early investigators that they were able to persuade farmers both to contribute data for cost analysis, and eventually to take part in more widely ranging survey work.

Once they had penetrated the barrier of suspicion and their bona fides had been accepted by cooperating farmers, the investigators had to confront the physical realities of travelling in rural Wales in the 1920s and 1930s. The local railway system was more extensive and more efficient than today's pitiful remnants. By contrast, though, thousands of miles of roads remained without tarmac surfaces so that travel by motorbike and car could often prove hazardous, especially when weather conditions were less than ideal. Besides, with filling stations and garages being few and far between, journeys beyond a few miles had to be planned with some care, a wise man always ensuring that a jerry can of petrol, some oil and possibly a spare fan belt was carried on board.

From today's standpoint of almost instant communication via email, mobile phone or text message, it is easy to forget the complexities of arranging visits to remote farms, many of which were not yet equipped with telephones. Letters had to be written (often in longhand due to shortage of secretarial help), reminders mailed and confirmatory telegrams despatched before the investigator set out for the farm. Having negotiated highways and byways and fords and potholes, the culmination of his journey was more often than not a bone-shaking rattle up a steep farm track. Journey's end, though, was merely the prelude to a series of formalities. As part of the exercise of building a relationship and maintaining confidence, investigators took care to enquire as to the health and happiness of family members and to mention mutual friends and acquaintances as they sipped their tea in the farmhouse kitchen. Dogs would be admired, horses critically evaluated and a new bull or piece of machinery learnedly discussed before the notepads and ledgers were eventually produced.

Given the relative crudeness of farmers' record keeping systems at the time, some skill was required to extract useable and analysable data from a mass of less relevant material. This applied in particular to financial information, much of it being presented in a miscellany of bills, invoices, cheque book stubs, notes taken at a market or sale, or even scraps of crumpled paper pulled from the inside pocket of an old jacket. Back at the office some sense had to be made of this apparent jumble of figures, and the initial procedure was to enter them onto large two feet square record cards for subsequent analysis. In the days before punched card systems became the norm and hand-operated calculators remained crude and expensive, analysis of data collected from a number of farms required laborious tabulation and lengthy and tedious arithmetical procedures. Moreover, as a result (in part of the universities' insistence upon strict independence on the part of the Advisory Economists), there was a tendency for the various Centres to develop their own methodologies and to present data after their own fashion.[26]

Analysis

Independence of methodology meant that in the case both of enterprise costings and whole farm surveys, data gathered by one Centre was not strictly comparable with that gathered elsewhere. As they became aware of this problem, a number of agricultural economists in the late 1920s began to discuss the possibility of formulating some sort of coordinated activity with respect to survey work. In 1922, a year after he had published his *Agricultural Atlas of Wales*, C.S. Orwin's colleague J. Pryse Howell produced *The Productivity of Hill Farming,* a study widely regarded as the first British example of a carefully conducted farm management survey.[27] From a methodological standpoint, Howell's work represented a complete departure from the well-worn route of cost accounting, and emphasised the value of the detailed survey as a means of forensically dissecting the economy of the farming sector. Howell's methodology, itself based on the approach evolved by American economists several decades previously, was soon adopted by others. Typically, the work of J.H. Venn and R.G. McCarslaw at Cambridge signalled further moves away from the technique of full individual farm costings towards the idea of collecting, by way of surveys, quantitative and financial data from as many farms as possible. Following surveys of sugar beet growing and bail milking, it soon became commonplace to apply the survey method as a means both of examining the anatomy of individual enterprises and of establishing the relative contributions of different enterprises to farm profitability.[28]

But these isolated studies, including the massive survey of 1,000 farms undertaken in the eastern counties by the Cambridge Provincial Centre, did little to resolve the issue of coordination.[29] This matter, above all, exercised the minds of the Conference of Provincial Agricultural Economists as they met regularly throughout the later 1920s and early 1930s.[30] After much discussion it was finally agreed that the best way forward would be for each Provincial Advisory Centre to collect and tabulate a set of basic data which would be sent to Oxford for further analysis by Orwin and his colleagues. Among the first fruits of the exercise was the National Milk Costs Investigation, initiated in 1934 and eventually continuing as the National Investigation into the Economics of Milk Production. This was followed in 1936 by the first of the annual National Farm Management Surveys, funded by the Treasury and continuing to operate (if in slightly different guise) to the present day.[31]

CHAPTER FIVE

The Development of the Survey, 1936–62

From Small Beginnings

IN PARALLEL WITH OTHER initiatives, including by now an impressive array of enterprise costings from the whole agricultural sector, the decision to coordinate some data analysis at Cambridge allowed agricultural economists to evolve a series of 'efficiency factors' by which individual farmers could evaluate the performance of their holdings alongside the average performance of a comparable group of producers. In effect, by the outbreak of the Second World War, farmers and agricultural advisors had access to an invaluable toolkit which remained a key indicator of standards until the development of gross margin analysis in the 1960s.[1]

Wartime Work and Staff Dispersal

The demands of the Farm Management Survey and a great deal of other more general accounting work required much time and effort on the part of Ashby, his Assistant Advisor, J. Pryse Howell, their statistical assistant J.R.E. Phillips and three clerical staff. The Aberystwyth contribution to the Farm Management Survey involved the collection and primary analysis of 60 accounting records and the survey returns from 140 farms throughout

Wales.[2] This apart, they collected and processed all the financial data associated with the Cahn Hill Improvement Scheme, that vast, extraordinary, and internationally important experiment carried out on the wild uplands above Devil's Bridge under the direction of R.G. Stapledon and Moses Griffith.[3] Concurrently A.E. Evans and J.D. Griffiths, assisted by J.H. Smith, squared up to the demands of the Milk Costs Investigation while E. Llewelyn Harry and W.H. Jones dealt with matters relating to advisory work in marketing. Aside from these core activities, advisory visits, and publishing studies of rural household budgeting, country markets, local milling and retail trading, the group managed, in 1936–7, to present 59 lectures and papers at meetings and conferences, and variously to sit on 24 extramural committees both in Wales and the rest of Britain.[4]

The outbreak of war spawned its own problems. As some individuals were called up for military service and others drafted onto the staffs of the various Welsh County War Agricultural Executive (Warag) Committees, Ashby fought hard to retain younger colleagues as call up papers landed on their doormats. Two of his most experienced men, E. Llewelyn Harry and W.H. Jones, had joined Warag Committees, the former serving as Executive Officer for Glamorgan for the whole of the war. When his senior clerical assistant announced his intention to volunteer for service with the RAF, Ashby concluded that further inroads into staff numbers would make it virtually impossible to carry out the volume of work expected by the Ministry of Agriculture, to say nothing of academic demands. Principal Ivor Evans was of the same mind and the two men succeeded in arguing that the nature of the work being carried out in the Department of Agricultural Economics demanded that staff be granted 'reserved occupation' status. In effect this secured a succession of temporary deferments of call-up for men like Joseph Smith, supervisor for the National Farm Survey for Wales and Monmouthshire and

J.R.E. Phillips and John David Griffiths, both heavily involved in the Farm Management Survey and the Milk Costs Investigation. Other staff, including Richard Bennett Jones, Charles Williams and Watkin Thomas, all of whom were considered vital to the operation of the Department, also managed for the moment to escape the call to arms.[5] Among their number was Brinley Campbell Jones, chief clerk of the general office and Ashby's personal assistant. In seeking complete reservation for Jones, who had served Ashby for 14 years, Principal Evans commended his extraordinary efficiency and the virtual impossibility of getting hold of a comparable replacement.

As the war years went on, Ashby had good reason to be thankful for the steadfast Jones upon whom he could rely to maintain the smooth day-to-day running of the secretariat during his many absences in London and elsewhere. Besides being a prominent member of the Central Agricultural Wages Board and sitting on a number of technical committees of the Ministry of Agriculture, Ashby was in constant demand as a speaker at venues throughout Britain. This not only took up a great deal of time, but also involved wrestling with the sometimes chaotic wartime railway timetables, to say nothing of the hazardous business of night time motoring on remote country roads during the 'blackout'. With his appointment in 1940 to the Scientific Committee of the War Cabinet's Food Policy Committee, established by Clement Attlee under the chairmanship of Sir William Bragg, President of the Royal Society, the shuttling to and fro to London only intensified.[6]

A National Survey

Once the war got fully underway, it became obvious to ministers that efficient management of the home food production campaign would be greatly enhanced by the accumulation of physical data for every farm in Britain, together with an assessment of the character and competence of its occupier. Valuable as the Farm Management Survey was, it did not permit the sort of broad surveillance deemed necessary at a time of national emergency. A rapid survey of British farming had been undertaken on a county basis in June 1940, but this was thought to be of little worth since inconsistency of data collection precluded inter-regional or inter-district comparison. A committee under the chairmanship of Sir Donald Ferguson, Permanent Secretary of the Ministry, had been set up to address this problem in late September and mandated to come up with immediately workable proposals. The committee, which included the celebrated geographer L. Dudley Stamp of the Land Utilisation Survey and the distinguished man of Welsh agricultural affairs, C. Bryner Jones, reported in December.[7] Anxious to avoid imposing further burdens on the already overstretched Warags, they proposed that additional data analysis be made the responsibility of the Advisory Economists and their staff at the various Provincial Centres. Their task would involve compiling a profile of each farm in the country in excess of five acres in size. Using the official June 4th Agricultural Returns, along with primary data collected on standardised record cards by investigators appointed by Warag District Committees, advisory staff would help to produce a comprehensive record of the state of productivity of each farm, together with a map of the holding.

This material would offer a basis for planning purposes besides pinpointing areas of potential improvement and identifying individual cases where farmers were dragging their heels. Among other things, it would allow the ready identification of 'C' farmers[8] who could be duly advised as to how they might improve their performance (see Chapter Two). The idea was for the advisory staff to compile much of the material in the offices of the County and District Warag Committees where copies of local June Returns were available together with the appropriate maps. The data would later be tabulated and analysed. Ferguson's committee fully realised that this project would involve the need for additional staff at the Provincial Centres and, in writing to each, he emphasised the desirability of appointing individuals who would be unlikely to be called up for military service.

When the committee's proposals arrived at Aberystwyth, Principal Evans and Ashby were quick to respond. Emphasising the formidable scale of the project which, they estimated, would involve in the region of 50,000 individual entries for Wales and Monmouthshire, they set out what they believed to be the minimum extra staffing requirements for the undertaking.[9] Under the watchful eye of Ashby himself, the project came to be supervised by Joseph Smith, at the time a technical assistant in the Department. As supervisor, Smith received £340 per annum and was assisted by a female 'indexer' (£200) and a clerical assistant along with five 'recorders' (£200) responsible for assembling data from the offices of the 13 County Committees.[10] While Smith liaised with the Warag District Committees and the recorders set about their work in the district offices, the indexer arranged the records as they arrived at Aberystwyth and created a file for each holding. The file contained both the primary material gathered by the District Committees and the June census material, and by way of a card index system a given holding could be rapidly identified. The assembled documentation, along with farm boundary maps, was then sampled and analysed to form the basis of a national statistical analysis of the farm survey data.[11] (Plate 25) Over the three years of the Survey, Ashby's Department received an extra annual subvention of £2,768 from the Ministry of Agriculture.

Plate 25. Extract from a 1936 farm survey recording sheet

A New Regime

As the war progressed and the Aberystwyth Provincial Advisory Centre laboured at the Farm Management Survey, the Milk Costs Investigation and the National Farm Survey, Ashby spent increasingly lengthy periods away from Cardiganshire in pursuance of his many official wartime duties. He was rewarded for his efforts with official recognition in the form of the C.B.E. and the offer of the Directorship of the Agricultural Economics Research Institute at the University of Oxford. Despite his affection for Wales, which remained undimmed to the end of his days, he accepted the offer and resigned from his Aberystwyth chair in 1946. After more than two decades, when he had occupied a prominent position both in the world of Welsh agriculture and the groves of academe at Aberystwyth, he left behind a powerful legacy of rigorous scholarship and a reputation of strict loyalty to his colleagues, all of whom held him in great affection. He was remembered by the farming world the length and breadth of Wales for his modesty, his quiet charm and his practical wisdom. His would, indeed, be a hard act to follow.

Ashby was succeeded by Eric F. Nash, a 41-year-old Oxford classicist and political economist who had held teaching posts in the USA and Canada and spent the pre-war years in the Ministry of Agriculture, where he was closely involved with the development of the Farm Management Survey and the Milk Costs Investigation. When war broke out, he was transferred to the Ministry of Food and worked alongside a group of outstanding agricultural economists including Sir Keith Murray, J.A. Raeburn and Ruth Cohen. Subsequently, he served as a member of the Control Commission for Germany which enabled him to expand further his experience of agricultural planning and to develop interests in the broad role of agriculture in national economies. Although, unlike Ashby, he had no personal connections with the farming industry, Nash had a deep understanding of the economics underlying agriculture and food production and supply.[12] A man of outstanding intellectual accomplishments, Nash challenged many of the basic assumptions of postwar agricultural policy and, indeed, of agricultural economics itself, and during his tenure of the Aberystwyth chair, he acquired the reputation of being something of an iconoclast. A stern critic of the conventional perception of agricultural protection, he sometimes came into conflict both with farmers and others in his profession who viewed agriculture as being rather more than a mere branch of applied economics. Being also a vigorous debater who did not suffer fools gladly, he became a somewhat isolated and rather formidable figure in Aberystwyth circles. Yet, to his departmental colleagues, he was a source of constant inspiration and during his 16 years as professor, the Department of Agricultural Economics continued to make notable contributions to the academic development of the subject.[13] Although incisive and analytical, Nash's own published output was limited, due in some measure to chronically poor health. However, he encouraged his staff to expand their academic vision to embrace the national and international aspects of agriculture in the economy so that the likes of E.A. Attwood, G. Hallett and R.G.C. McCrone published widely on the broader structural issues and the relationship between British and European agriculture.

For all his many qualities, Nash had little time for what he regarded as non-academic research and the somewhat humdrum business of survey work and farm enterprise studies demanded by contractual obligations with the Ministry of Agriculture.[14] Indeed, like some other Aberystwyth academics, he tended to regard many of the staff engaged in the former activities as belonging to the ranks of lesser mortals until they showed some positive evidence of scholarly ability. This probably rankled, and in any case was hardly fair. After all, W. Dyfri Jones, M.H. Dummer, M.B. Jawetz, J.R.E. Phillips and M. Morgan Rees put the results of Farm Management Survey work to good effect in a series of studies of the economics of poultry production, hill sheep, the dairy industries and seed potatoes, published by the Department.[15]

J. Pryse Howell, however, did not count among the lesser mortals. Held in the highest regard by Principal Ivor Evans, Howell also enjoyed the respect and admiration of both the Welsh farming community and the mandarins of Whitehall. In May 1946, J.H. Kirk, at the time a senior official in the Ministry of Agriculture, wrote to Evans of Howell's

> ... extremely valuable services over a long period, not only to the University College, but to the Ministry and the farmers of Wales. In this office we are fully appreciative of his standing as one of the pioneers of agricultural economics in this country, and being for the most part younger men, realise how much in our current work we are resting on foundations which Howell and a few others of his generation of agricultural economists have so firmly laid.[16]

Howell's considerable reputation and personal standing gave Nash the ideal opportunity to leave the totality of the advisory and commissioned work of the Department under the former's immediate supervision, much to the delight of Principal Evans. Having persuaded the Ministry to raise Howell's salary to that equivalent to an Independent Lecturer, the Principal advised him that, "… your experience and knowledge of Welsh farming must, I am sure, be fully utilised if this work is to be successfully carried out".[17] Howell discharged the task with distinction until his retirement in 1952.

The minutes of the College Staffing Committee for May 1951, set out a profile both of Howell and the rest of the established academic members of the advisory staff under Nash's direction. They are summarised below.

Name	Age	Date of appointment	Status	Salary
J. Pryse Howell	63	October 1925	Senior Scientific Officer	£895 + £105 bonus
J.R.E. Phillips	41	January 1935	Senior Agricultural Economist	£760 + £90 bonus
A.M.M. Rees	26	November 1948	Agricultural Economist	£470 + £90 bonus
M.H. Dummer	30	September 1949	Assistant Agricultural Economist	£395 + £88 bonus
C.J. Lewis	26	August 1950	Assistant Agricultural Economist	£295 + £78 bonus
E. Williams	32	September 1950	Assistant Agricultural Economist	£370 + £82 bonus
Dyfri Jones	27	September 1948	Assistant Agricultural Economist	£345 + £78 bonus

A Change of Title

Once the war was over and those agricultural economists who had been seconded to the Ministry of Agriculture and elsewhere had returned to their academic institutions, they were confronted with a potentially serious change in their role and status. With the creation of the National Agricultural Advisory Service the strategic decision was taken to detach the Provincial Advisory Service, with its soil scientists, bacteriologists, chemists and agriculturalists, from the universities and to place them under the direct control of the Ministry of Agriculture. It was the initial intention to include the agricultural economists among this grouping. The prospect of becoming full-time civil servants, however, with all that that implied for academic integrity and farmer confidentiality, had little appeal for senior members of the profession and they set about persuading the Ministry to seek an alternative route. It was eventually agreed, though not without a certain amount of vigorous argument, that the 250 agricultural economists would be located at nine academic institutions where they would comprise the Provincial Agricultural Economics Service. By retaining the Provisional Agricultural Economist and those of his staff involved with the Farm Management Survey in the academic sector, the Ministry was assured of obtaining independent and unbiased advice, a matter of vital importance insofar as the Annual Price Review was concerned.

Principal Ivor Evans of Aberystwyth and his long-time friend and collaborator Arthur Ashby had been among the foremost lobbyists for retaining the by now traditional association of the Universities with the burgeoning discipline of agricultural economics. Not surprisingly, therefore, Evans was delighted to learn of the eventual decision in favour of doing so. The Ministry of Agriculture, he was told, was keen "… fully to preserve the functions and status of the Provincial Agricultural Economists, and the relationship which they have developed with cooperating farmers". Moreover, although the National Agricultural Advisory Service might eventually appoint their own farm management staff, this would in no way, "… prejudice or hold up any developments which the Universities may be planning in the field of farm management, if they feel as we do, that there is also room for expansion in this branch of agricultural economics under University auspices".[18] The cost of the service would continue to be supported by direct grant from the Treasury by way of the Ministry of Agriculture.[19]

Continuing Wrangles

The establishment of the new service was received with less than universal acclamation by staff at the University in Aberystwyth. Even with the passing of the years there remained, and remains to this day, an incipient tension between members of the conventional academic departments and the agricultural economists, who continued to be viewed by some as lesser breeds beyond the law. The gulf was emphasised in differences in salaries, status and promotion prospects between the two groups and, as is so often the case with money matters, the disparity deepened the rivalry and fomented the bitterness. Nash and his professorial colleagues at other institutions strove vigorously to persuade universities, colleges and the Ministry of Agriculture to recognise the anomaly and to assimilate the staff of the Provincial Agricultural Economics Service (PAES) into the university salary system. At Aberystwyth, Nash encouraged both individuals and groups to write to the University authorities over the issue. When Pryse Howell, J.R.E. Phillips and Mostyn Dummer did so in June of 1951, they were awarded ex officio payments, although no formal arrangements were made.[20] Several years later, however, Nash was asked by the Ministry of Agriculture to nominate individuals within the PAES whom he considered to be of 'academic' and 'non-academic' calibre.[21] This seems to have been the prelude to assimilation to university grades which eventually occurred in October 1956, by which time Nash's team included four lecturers, three assistant lecturers, one senior investigation officer and nine investigation officers. Of the total staff complement, the professor and one lecturer were funded by the University and the remainder by the Ministry of Agriculture. Mr Napolitan, the senior civil servant in the Ministry responsible for handling negotiations, emphasised to

Principal Thomas Parry, who had recently succeeded Ivor Evans, that the primary purpose of the assimilation exercise had been to remove any differentiation in status and position between the PAES and other staff of the University.[22] By way of clarification of the post-assimilation position, the Ministry issued a detailed memorandum in May 1959, setting out unequivocally the threefold roles of the PAES within the university framework:

(a) to undertake and participate as required in the university's research work,

(b) to give specialist economic advice to farmers and advisory officers, and

(c) to conduct investigations into farm incomes and costs as requested by the Ministry.[23]

With the departure of the Welsh Plant Breeding Station to Plas Gogerddan near Bow Street in 1953, there followed an unseemly inter-departmental wrangle as to the use of the agriculture building on the Penglais site.[24] The outcome of this rather distasteful episode was the enforced withdrawal of the Department of Agricultural Economics from the building and its relocation to the insalubrious and gloomy environs of Cambrian Chambers in Aberystwyth. It seemed to some that just as the University had come to recognise the worth of agricultural economics as a subject, its practitioners were despatched to the academic nether regions, out of sight and even out of mind. This illogical separation of the economists from colleagues in the other agricultural subjects incensed Professor Nash, and he was quick to pick up Ashby's standard and engage with the authorities in a lengthy struggle to secure more acceptable accommodation for his Department. In this endeavour he had the wholehearted support of the Ministry of Agriculture whose officers regarded Cambrian Chambers as being quite inadequate both for the teaching department and the PAES. As one official wrote to Nash, the terms of the Ministry grant stated unequivocally that the University had full responsibility for accommodating the PAES and he hoped that in its future accommodation plans it would not 'discriminate' against the Department.[25] Although an increasingly sick man, Nash stuck to his guns and missed few opportunities to lobby for a decent building for his Department. But it was to be his last struggle, and four years would elapse after his death in 1962 before his colleagues moved back to Penglais to take their rightful places alongside their scientific brethren.[26]

Towards the Present

Following the untimely death of Eric Nash, the Department of Agricultural Economics came briefly under the supervision of D.H. Evans and J.R.E. Phillips, of whom the latter undertook temporary responsibility for Ministry contract work. In the meantime the Chair of Agricultural Economics was advertised. From the nine applicants, W.J. Thomas of the University of Manchester was selected, but after some consideration he decided to decline the offered post. This left the selection committee with something of a predicament and, when they met in London in the agreeable surroundings of the Athenaeum to discuss the way forward, one of the Ministry of Agriculture representatives suggested that the University might care to consider the name of Huw T. Williams. Williams had begun undergraduate life as a geographer, before graduating from Aberystwyth in 1933 with a degree in economics. He had subsequently worked in the Agricultural Economics Research Institute at Reading University before being drafted into the Ministry of Agriculture in 1940. Here, he had been closely involved in drawing up the ground-breaking 1947 Agriculture Act and, as Head of the Economics and Statistics branch of the Ministry, in creating the structural framework of the PAES. Alongside his wide experience of agricultural administration, Williams had established his teaching bona fides as Deputy Principal of Seale-Hayne Agricultural

College in Devon.[27] Seeing a way out of their present dilemma, the selection committee took up the Ministry's suggestion and the Principal was authorised to interview Williams with the aim of offering him the vacant Chair. There was, he was warned, a challenging time ahead as the Department faced growing competition from other centres. But Williams was not the man to turn away from a challenge and, in the autumn of 1964, he returned to Aberystwyth to head the Department of Agricultural Economics for the next 13 years. (Plate 26)

Plate 26. Huw T. Williams, Professor of Agricultural Economics, 1964–76

Together at Last

Within a month or so of Williams's appointment, the Department received a visitation from the influential Cohen Committee which was reviewing the activities of the PAES and seeking to identify 'growth points' in the service. The Committee was impressed by the high calibre of the PAES investigational officers who were more than capable of discharging their duties without undue recourse to the academic staff. Many of the latter though, expressed their misgivings over the 'costings chore', claiming that this aspect of their work limited scope for advanced teaching and research.[28] Miss Cohen and her colleagues noted these observations and in any case had probably heard them rehearsed in other centres. The Cohen Committee's deliberations had two highly significant consequences. Of major importance from the standpoint of Aberystwyth was the designation of the University as one of the six 'growth points' for teaching and research in agricultural economics in Great Britain. Secondly, the Committee recommended that the funding of the PAES be transferred from the Ministry of Agriculture to the University Grants Committee over the quinquennium 1967–72. In effect, all investigational work on behalf of the Ministry would now be carried out on a contractual basis, with the Ministry providing supplementary grants to fund promising fields of research. This second outcome met with the wholehearted approval of most agricultural economists in Britain, some of whom had campaigned for the transfer of funding since the assimilation of PAES staff onto university salary grades a decade previously. After 40 years in the semi-wilderness, those agricultural economists not previously funded by the University could now look forward to full integration into its affairs.[29]

CHAPTER SIX

The Farm Business Survey – Towards the Present

Moving Ahead

BETWEEN THE MID-1960s AND late 1970s, the Department of Agricultural Economics at Aberystwyth enjoyed a period of steady growth and development. Student numbers at both undergraduate and postgraduate level expanded and research and consultancy activity widened to embrace overseas development, European agricultural economics and, in particular, marketing studies and agricultural cooperation. H.T. Williams himself staunchly championed the cause of agricultural marketing, and worked strenuously in support of the Welsh Agricultural Organisation Society, the parent body of agricultural cooperation in Wales. It was due, in large measure, to his lobbying efforts that the funds became available from the National Farmers Union Development Trust and elsewhere for the establishment of a Chair in Agricultural Marketing in the Department. As an initial move, a senior lectureship was established and the first professorial appointment made in 1979, three years after Williams's retirement.[1]

In the meantime, the pressures of undertaking commissioned work for the Ministry of Agriculture continued to cause some concern and to absorb a growing proportion of Departmental resources.[2] Nevertheless, the Provincial Agricultural Economics Service (PAES) was receiving almost £50,000 annually from the Ministry during the mid-1960s, while survey and costings data provided an invaluable resource for detailed studies of the economic and social state of farming in Wales, of regional variations in farm incomes and of the economic problems of hill farming areas. The PAES, moreover, provided a database for the National Agricultural Advisory Service (NAAS) whose officers drew heavily upon it when drawing up advisory programmes.[3] For some years prior to his appointment to a lectureship in the Department in 1971, Michael Haines had served as district officer for the NAAS both in Newtown and Carmarthen. In this capacity, he attended meetings of the Technical Development Committee in the late 1960s and he paid warm tribute to the skills and strength of character of Mostyn Dummer and M.B. Jawetz, one or other of whom gave a yearly presentation of the Farm Management Survey results to the Committee. Jawetz spent a brief period as farm management liaison officer before being succeeded in that office by Dummer and Dyfri Jones. Jawetz and Dummer, and later Dyfri Jones, were responsible for ensuring that the Ministry of Agriculture received Survey returns in the form of 'broadsheets', large sheets of ruled and cross ruled paper containing data for a single farm. At a later stage Dyfri Jones helped to develop tabular systems which ultimately metamorphosed into computer print outs which were submitted to the Ministry.[4] These men successively served as key points of contact between the Survey and the continually evolving NAAS, ensuring the development of a mutually fruitful relationship. The Survey was taken very seriously both by NAAS and the farming community and participating farmers viewed their association with the University with pride and satisfaction. In later years, as a lecturer and subsequently Professor and Head of Department, Haines strove to build upon the reserve of goodwill developed among Welsh farmers to evolve a wide network of valuable contacts. (Plate 27) Over time, this would result in practical and financial support from the farming community for teaching and research, along with a variety of external consultancy activities redounding to the credit of the University. Although sometimes sneered upon by conventional academe, consultancy work and the compilation of reports based upon carefully gathered evidence was an important component of the work of agriculturally-orientated university departments at this time. Haines's appointment, along with two other academics, Bernard Delagneau and D.A.G. Green, was initially funded by the Ministry of Agriculture after a strong case for additional staff had been made by H.T. Williams. So it was that the Department increased its academic component at no cost to the University. Green, for example, took no part in the affairs of the Survey until his appointment as its Director in 1978.[5]

By way of simplifying administration and offering greater flexibility in resource allocation, the respective funding of the Department's activities was split between the Ministry of

Plate 27. Michael Haines, Professor of Agricultural Marketing and Head of Department, 1995–2000

Agriculture and the University Grants Committee (UGC) in August 1968. Henceforth, purely academic work would come under the aegis of the UGC while the PAES would be funded entirely by the Ministry. This would continue to remain the position until 1979 when the Welsh Office's Agriculture Department replaced the Ministry of Agriculture as the commissioning authority.[6]

Out and About

As systems of funding and other administrative matters were being discussed in smoke-filled rooms in the Ministry of Agriculture, investigational officers and clerical staff worked steadily at the job in hand. Roads may have improved, cars may have become more reliable and farm lanes less damaging to chassis and spine, yet the basic task of collecting information differed little in the 1970s from 30 years previously. Different areas of the country were allocated to individual investigational officers (or 'the men from Aberystwyth' as they became known in farming circles), each of whom organised his own timetable. Given the size of Wales relative to the number of investigational officers, an individual sometimes needed to remain away from home for up to a week at a time as he located and visited his client farmers.[7] The drive up the farm track was the prelude to a day of mingled pleasure and frustration, the relative proportions of each depending upon how effectively an individual farmer organised his accounts and related papers. The eventual imposition of Value Added Tax forced farmers into keeping reasonably systematised accounts, thereby easing the investigational officer's task.[8] Previously, though, data gathering was a more challenging affair as invoices were liberated from coat hangers, chequebook stubs pulled out from behind plates on laden dressers and crumpled paying in books discovered in the most unlikely of places. One way or another, this material had to be forged into some sort of order and the first stage was to enter all available details by hand into green jacketed account books, a process which could easily take up much of the day. Some farmers would already have partially completed the 'green book', others would sit by while the investigational officer set about the business, while others yet would leave him to his own devices. But, however laborious this task may have been, it was tempered by the pleasures of friendship, of shared interests and of wide ranging conversation at various times of the day. (Plate 28)

As the 'man from Aberystwyth' became increasingly familiar within the local area, he became almost a member of the family and his visits would be eagerly awaited by children and anticipated with pleasure by grown-ups. The day would be punctuated by plentiful cups of tea and coffee and an ample lunch, during

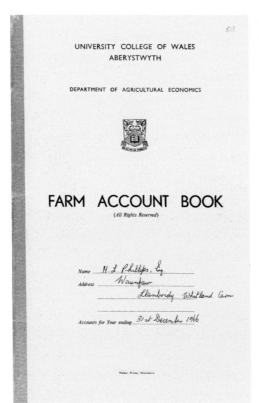

Plate 28. A typical 'green book' from 1966

UNIVERSITY COLLEGE OF WALES
ABERYSTWYTH

DEPARTMENT OF AGRICULTURAL ECONOMICS

FARM ACCOUNT BOOK
(All Rights Reserved)

Name *H. L. Phillips, Esq.*
Address *Waunfawr*
Llanboidy Whitland Carm

Accounts for Year ending *31st December 1966*

which the farming world would be put to rights, mutual friends and acquaintances would be discussed and local issues debated. Over time the relationship between the investigational officer and his client farmers developed into one of mutual trust and, in some cases, of close friendship. Such interpersonal confidence was essential to the success of the whole enterprise.[9] Being conservative by nature, farmers as a whole were unlikely to warm to an investigational officer whose dress sense tended towards the bizarre. Dyed hair, earrings and multicoloured kaftans may have been *de rigueur* for an audition for a part in a Gilbert and Sullivan operetta, but for a farm visit these excesses of adornment just would not do! A man's dress needed to be conventional as his knowledge of practical farming needed to be sound.[10]

'Green books' completed and farewells made, the investigational officer returned to Aberystwyth. At this point it was the turn of the predominantly female clerical staff to wrestle with the accumulated material. Handling and organising data in the pre-computer era required a good deal of sheer physical effort, and it is only too easy to forget the skill and precision demanded of clerical staff at the time. Although the early Burroughs calculators had largely been replaced by more sophisticated electronic machines by the 1970s, there still remained plenty of hand tabulation and calculation to be undertaken once the raw data from sampled farms arrived at the clerical office.[11] This material had to be typed and transferred to profit or loss statements, and data had to be tabulated and forwarded to the general office for collation before reports were written.

Computerisation, of course, would eventually revolutionise data handling. In the early stages of computerisation, however, the process remained laborious and time-consuming as figures from the green books were transferred to data sheets and thence to punched cards before being processed by computer at Manchester University. With the arrival of a mainframe computer on the University campus in the mid-1980s, it became possible to process all Farm Management Survey material in Aberystwyth itself. This was largely facilitated by the efforts of the recently-appointed computer officer, N.D.H. Chapman, who created suitable software both for card reading and for delivering analysed data and reports. Chapman's skills, coupled with those of Huw Williams, a highly capable investigational officer and computer user who joined the survey in 1985, were later recruited to adapt data processing to the application of personal computers which made their appearance in the next decade. Henceforth punched cards would become redundant as information was transferred directly from handwritten sheets to the computer, or, rather later, from raw data collected on farm visits to the hard drive of a laptop computer.[12] After many years the 'green book' was almost consigned to history.[13]

In the meantime clerical assistants had to despatch copies of Survey results to cooperating farmers and deal with all manner of routine correspondence. Besides, in the 1980s and 1990s other commissioned surveys and studies were being pursued in parallel with the farm income work. The National Survey of the Economics of Milk Production, studies of the economics of beef, pig and poultry production, to say nothing of the massive Hill and Uplands Research Project of the early 1980s, all imposed further work for clerical staff attached to the Survey.[14]

A Visitation and Some Restructuring

For many years those applied agricultural economists who had used Survey data as the basis of publications produced 'in-house' or printed in the periodical literature, had been criticised by some economists working in the more abstract and theoretical areas of the subject. There was, however, no such criticism from working agricultural economists who had long adopted this form of publication, both at Aberystwyth and in other university departments of agricultural economics. Worthy and useful though their work may have been, it was claimed that it had made little contribution to the development of the conceptual basis of agricultural economics as an academic discipline. To a degree, this view was confirmed by the UGC Sub-Committee on Agricultural Economics, chaired by Sir Kenneth Berrill, which reported in May 1970. The PAES, the Sub-Committee noted, had been a major factor in the stimulation of interest in agricultural economics at university level. Nevertheless, the Sub-Committee could not but observe that 'the routine nature' of commissioned work may have resulted, "… particularly before 1957, in less stringent scrutiny of needs before academic appointments were approved, and in application of less exacting standards of selection". In other words, "… the PAES system may thus have generated academic activities of a quality and value which might not otherwise have been undertaken".[15] This was a general observation and not specifically directed towards Aberystwyth, yet it is not difficult to imagine the disquiet with which it was greeted by several members, including Mostyn Dummer, W. Dyfri Jones and J.R.E. Phillips (who had joined the Department in 1935) who had based much of their earlier work on survey and costings data. They may have kept their feelings to themselves, but they must have felt both distressed and humiliated by the implications of Berrill's report.[16]

As part of a general restructuring exercise within the University, the School of Agricultural Sciences was created in the late 1960s and from the outset the Department of Agricultural Economics became part of this academic grouping. Viewed by the UGC as a 'growth area', the Department was enabled to make a series of key appointments in both the general area of agricultural economics and in the burgeoning field of agricultural marketing and marketing management. When H.T. Williams retired in 1976, he was succeeded by D.I. Bateman, a graduate of the University of Liverpool, who had been a member of the department since 1963, having previously served in the Economics Department of the Milk Marketing Board.[17] (Plate 29) The subsequent appointments of P.J. Baron and his successor Michael Haines as Professors of Agricultural Marketing allowed the Department to develop further strong links with the agricultural and allied industries which supplemented and strengthened the contacts with practical farming maintained by way of 'commissioned work' for the Ministry of Agriculture.

Commissioned work helped to meet Departmental costs and to provide valuable 'spin off' material for research, besides helping to finance short-term appointments. On the other hand, the demand for commissioned studies was so great by the early 1980s that staff numbers proved inadequate and some projects had to be turned down or delayed.[18] The Ministry of Agriculture (and subsequently the Welsh Office) funded six investigational officers and a similar number of clerical staff and although these personnel were able to

Plate 29. David I. Bateman, Professor of Agricultural Economics, 1976–94

meet the demands of the Survey, they were hard-pushed to deal with the requirements of other commissions. To some extent the difficulty was surmounted by the appointment of short-term researchers linked to specific projects. By this means a great deal of work was undertaken, some of it drawing upon the resources of the Survey. G.O. Hughes's wide-ranging study of Welsh net farm income in the early 1980s (which eventually became incorporated within a government White Paper) embodied Survey data, while the same author's work on the impact of environmental initiatives on farm incomes, undertaken in collaboration with T.N. Jenkins, also drew upon this valuable source.[19] In terms of attracting external funding it could be argued that the 1980s and 1990s were the culmination of the Survey's success. As the National Survey of the Economics of Milk Production monitored the effects of recently-introduced milk quotas and the Hill Cattle and Sheep Survey became fully integrated into the Farm Management Survey, other studies were initiated. These included investigations of the early potato industry and the farm machinery business and a major contribution to a review of beef production in Britain coordinated by Manchester University.[20] It is probable that the proven track record of the Survey in delivering unbiased and reliable financial data over many years was the magnet attracting so much commissioned work to Aberystwyth in these fruitful decades. The Ministry of Agriculture and the various official and unofficial bodies which turned to the Department could do so in the sure knowledge not only of the skills of its researchers but of their appreciation of the needs and nuances of the Welsh farming community. That community, in turn, respected the role of the Survey and readily cooperated in its diverse endeavours. Perhaps not surprisingly, the Survey directly impacted in a positive way on the teaching activities of the Department of Agricultural Economics. Students pursuing courses in the economics of farm business management regularly visited cooperating farms, while the Department's growing contingent of overseas students from Africa and Asia derived great benefit from contact with working farmers engaged with the Survey.[21]

A New Name

As heads of the Department of Agricultural Economics, both H.T. Williams and D.I. Bateman shouldered overall responsibility for the work of the Survey.[22] Day-to-day management, however, was left in the hands of another member of staff. For a number of years the task was undertaken by Dyfri Jones who had been farm business liaison officer before 'assimilation', and by 1971 was a senior lecturer in the Department. The spring of the same year saw the appointment of D.A.G. Green as lecturer in agricultural economics. Having spent three years as an investigational officer at King's College, University of Durham

Plate 30. David A. G. Green, Senior Lecturer in Agricultural Economics and Survey Director, 1978–88

before attending the Universities of Kentucky and Michigan State, Green succeeded Dyfri Jones as Director of the Survey in 1978 and continued in this capacity for ten years.[23] (Plate 30)

Over the course of the two previous decades the nature of the agricultural industry had been changing in a variety of ways. Heavy capital investment, intensification, rising land values and the capricious nature of the national economy meant that farming was becoming ever-more complex. It was no longer enough merely to master the technical knowledge required for efficient farming, but the farmer needed to understand and embrace a variety of business management skills. In order to reflect this vital change, the orientation of the Farm Management Survey changed in various subtle ways and in 1985 it was reborn as the Farm Business Survey.[24] In the process of reorientating the Survey, the Ministry of Agriculture's statisticians closely scrutinised the sample of collaborating farmers and noted that a disproportionate number had been involved for many years. Concerned that this would lead to 'conditioning' and thus to a degree of bias, they decreed that the sample should be subject to a ten per cent turnover each year. In other words, of the 500 Welsh farms surveyed, 50 would be annually replaced by alternative holdings drawn from the centrally-maintained National Farm Census. If this made sound statistical sense, it created a great deal of extra work for investigational officers.[25] Letters had to be written to selected farmers who were then visited and the nature and conduct of the Survey explained to them in detail. Whether or not a given farmer accepted the invitation to take part depended in large measure on the persuasiveness of the officer in pressing the benefits of membership of the Survey. As time went by initial arrangements came to be carried out on the telephone, although exploratory farm visits were and still are undertaken.

For a brief period in the early 1990s the Department of

Agricultural Economics was amalgamated with her sister Department of Economics. The marriage, however, proved less than convivial, and by 1993 key personnel in the area of applied economics and agricultural marketing chose to move to the newly formed Department of Agricultural Sciences, a grouping created in response to the 1992 Research Assessment Exercise. Although many years had passed since the Department of Agricultural Economics had moved from Cambrian Chambers to the Penglais site with its sumptuous views and sylvan surroundings, it seemed somehow fated to be, like the *Flying Dutchman*, forever on the move. No sooner had the dust of the journey from the Llandinam to the Cledwyn Building settled, when another merger loomed on the near horizon. The lengthy, tortuous and often tedious negotiations over the proposed merger of the Department of Agricultural Sciences with the Welsh Agricultural College were coming towards their close and the decision to locate the merged institution on the Llanbadarn campus heralded yet further change. Within two years the Survey would be housed in the rather dreary 1970s brutalist building on the latter campus.

Yet More Change

On 8 June 1993, Professor David Bateman, in his capacity as Research Director of the Department of Agricultural Sciences, received a letter from the Welsh Office whose contents, according to the signatory, "... will cause you great concern".[26] In accordance with the Conservative government's insistence that all official goods and services be acquired by competitive tender, the letter announced, existing contracts between the Farm Business Survey and the Welsh Office would eventually be terminated and new arrangements formulated. In effect, the survival of the Survey in the future would be partially, if not wholly, dependent upon the success of its senior officers in drawing up suitable tenders.

D.A.G. Green's directorship had come to an end in 1988 and in due course he was succeeded by T.N. Jenkins who confronted the tendering issue and successfully orchestrated the affairs of the Survey while concurrently producing a series of influential publications in the area of developmental economics.[27] (Plate 31)

In 2003, however, Jenkins left the university and the directorial reins were taken up by Anthony O'Regan, an agricultural graduate, trained accountant and practical farmer. The various structural changes taking place in the University, including the creation of the Welsh Institute of Rural Sciences and subsequently the Institute of Biological, Environmental and Rural Sciences, markedly altered the overall academic balance within the agricultural subject area. In the mid-1990s, before the retirement of Bateman and Haines and the transfer of key senior staff to the School of Business Studies, there had been at least 15 members of academic staff on the Llanbadarn campus with a direct interest in the discipline of agricultural economics. Such

Plate 31 Tim N. Jenkins, Senior Research Associate and Survey Director, 1988–2003

has been the decline of the subject at Aberystwyth that at the time of writing there are but three rural economists/lecturers in the newly-created Institute of Biological, Environmental and Rural Sciences, one of whom is O'Regan himself.[28] (Plate 32) Under his able supervision, the Survey entered a brave new world of open competitive tendering, which required, and requires, close engagement with government objectives and European legistlation. After successfully retaining the contract, and a number of extensions and subsequent renewals, he followed what was now becoming a customary task for Survey Directors, and oversaw the relocation of the staff from the Llanbadarn campus to the former Institute of Grassland and Environmental Research (IGER) site at Gogerddan, near Bow Street.[29] This might seem somewhat ironic since the Survey had formerly cohabited with IGER's predecessor, the Welsh Plant Breeding Station, some 75 years earlier! In addition to his other academic responsibilities O'Regan presently oversees a Survey consisting of a contingent of nine investigational officers and

Plate 32. Tony O'Regan, director of the Farm Business Survey, 2003–present

two clerical assistants, their efforts continuing to be underpinned by the computational expertise of N.D.H. Chapman and D.H. Williams. (See Appendices I and II)

The Survey Today

The Annual Price Review, of course, has long since disappeared. Nevertheless the Welsh Farm Business Survey continues to be an essential component of the various elements employed in determining agricultural and rural strategy. Income data from the several and varied sectors of the agricultural industry is essential to the accurate setting of levels of farm support, the extent of environmental payments and a wide range of both short and longer term strategic considerations. Besides, the information collected from the 550 farms in the Welsh Survey feeds into the regular pan-European farm surveys whereby the Brussels bureaucrats gather evidence for strategic planning.

In more recent years, the considerable capacity of the Survey to deliver supplementary information has been officially recognised. In this respect a great deal of the material collected by investigational officers at Aberystwyth contributes to detailed studies undertaken by specialist staff both in the Welsh Assembly Government and in Whitehall. Animal health, farm water sources, agricultural carbon footprints and the overall quality of farm management are but a few examples of these areas of activity. As society is forced to come to grips with the inevitabilities of climate change and population growth, it is probable that core data from the Survey will be of seminal importance in the future. Farmers' attitudes towards these problems and their preparedness (or otherwise) to modify practices in the light of climatic and environmental change need urgently to be determined across the totality of the agricultural industry. Establishing attitudes and intentions prior to allocating resources may well bring about substantial savings to Exchequer and taxpayer.

From an operational standpoint, the Farm Business Survey has experienced a number of significant changes over the past decade. Seventy-five years ago the investigational officer doubled as an advisor to his client farmers. But the dual activities of collecting data for official purposes and concurrently giving advice, led almost inevitably to sample bias so that the advisory function eventually fell into abeyance. Today's investigational officer is specifically prohibited from offering advice or guidance under the terms of the contract agreed with the Welsh Assembly Government. His task, both on or off the farm, has been ameliorated by developments in electronic technology, so that he can now collect and tabulate data with an ease and precision undreamt of by his predecessors. Even so, and as in all walks of life, as tasks become easier the quantity of tasks tends to increase. In this respect the Survey is no different. Once collected, data is now transmitted electronically to the Welsh Assembly Government and to the Duchy College in Cornwall where it is included for analysis in the full United Kingdom Farm Business Survey.

Annual printed reports of the Welsh Farm Business Survey continue to be produced by the University with the *Statistical Results* volume representing a continuation of the *Farm Incomes in Wales* publications of former decades. The latter offered summaries of the financial results of the different categories of Welsh farms along with a brief report and commentary on the general state of the industry in that particular year. The results of the Survey were originally expressed on a per farm and per 100-acre basis, with average and above average levels of performance identified for each farm type. These offered farmers and advisors a set of management standards by which they could evaluate the performance of a particular business. As recording and analysis became more sophisticated and the distinction between overhead and variable costs recognised, details of sectoral farm incomes were published alongside enterprise gross margins and other valuable diagnostic data.

The present *Statistical Results* volumes contain a series of tables of inter year comparisons of identical samples of farms within different enterprise and size categories. They provide details of input/output data, farm incomes and gross margins, together with other material relating to farm productivity including land utilisation, tenants' capital investment and levels of assets and liabilities. Taken together, the *Statistical Results* and *Farm Incomes in Wales* publications comprise a body of statistical material which may eventually prove invaluable to historians of the agriculture of Wales in the second half of the twentieth century. Moreover, they are a valuable and readily accessible resource to academics, economists and advisors. On the other hand, as O'Regan readily admits, the *Statistical Results* are rather unwieldy and less than 'farmer friendly'. To circumvent this problem he has initiated the production of a bilingual pocket-sized booklet which summarises annual farm incomes and gross margins for the principal enterprises. Sponsored by the 'Farming Connect' scheme and the Welsh Assembly Government, this booklet is mailed to some 40,000 farmers and farming-related individuals in Wales and has significantly raised the profile of the Survey among the farming body as a whole.[30] In so doing, it has further enhanced the reputation of the University at Aberystwyth which has taken pride in its close relationship with the broader Welsh community since its origins in the 1870s. There have been awkward moments and the occasional alarums and excursions, yet the University has consistently supported the activities of the Survey for three quarters of a century. The Survey draws strength from its close association with the University, while participating farmers are secure in the knowledge that their financial affairs will be treated confidentially and with complete impartiality. Valued relationships have been forged over many years in an atmosphere of mutual trust and respect. At a time when public confidence in political organisations is at a low ebb and when many formerly hallowed institutions are the subject of rigorous critical scrutiny, there is every reason to continue to cherish and nurture an enterprise widely recognised as beyond reproach. People will come and go and methodologies will change, but is to be hoped that when the Survey celebrates its centenary in 2036, it will continue do so as a valued unit within the University at Aberystwyth.[31]

CHAPTER SEVEN

The Survey as a Resource for Historians

Value of Everything, Cost of Nothing

FOR CENTURIES BEFORE THE birth of the Farm Business Survey, farmers were reckoned, to paraphrase Oscar Wilde, to know the value of everything, but the cost of nothing. Throughout society in general, the pendulum may recently have swung the other way although there can be little doubt that in the farming world as a whole, cost, price and value have long since been of absolute concern to producers.

Like any commercial activity, the purpose of a farm business is to create value and to do so in such a manner that someone, be it the market, state or a generous benefactor, is willing to supply money in exchange. And herein lies the difficulty. Unless the farmer has a full record of the resources consumed by the actions of creating the value, it becomes extremely difficult for he or she to determine what is an acceptable price for a given product at which production might be continued. Besides, a myriad of extraneous factors beyond the farmer's control can come into the equation which, in themselves, tend to engender a cautious attitude. Moreover, even today, a person skilled in animal and crop husbandry whose quotidian life is determined by the vagaries of wind and weather may well take a jaundiced view of the glib blandishments of laptop toting financial advisors. It is hardly surprising then, that selling the benefits of quality financial data to a needy and hard-bitten industry was always likely to be a long haul. But, it eventually proved remarkably successful and by the later twentieth and early twenty-first centuries a rich harvest of profit forecasts, gross margins, breakeven budgets, performance indicators and benchmarks had been garnered. This massive accumulation of performance data and Survey material offers an invaluable resource base and provides unprecedented opportunities for both agricultural and social historians.

Snags and Pitfalls

Historians are forever in pursuit of contemporary original documents. The art historian, for example, will seek a painter's sketches, cartoons and notes so as to piece together the thinking underlying the creative process. Meanwhile the biographer will look to letters, diaries and similar material so as to reconstruct the lives of his subject and those close to him or her. Similar sorts of primary sources may also be important to economic historians or historians of business or agriculture, although for them, a continuous run of statistical data covering a lengthy period of time is every bit as valuable. Not only are long and consistent runs of statistics relatively rare, but they usually demand very cautious interpretation. They may offer potentially rich pickings, but those working with them need to be alive to the snags and pitfalls awaiting the unwary.

Take, for example, the wholly hypothetical case of a ledger purporting to record the average weight of cattle sold at Cardiff Fair between 1750 and 1850. One might think that such a run of data would enable reflections on aspects of genetic change among local cattle over a longish period of time. (Plate 33) But even if we ignore the obvious issues of nutrition and environment as determinants of weight, many other questions need to be posed before the material can be approached with any degree of confidence. How were the animals weighed and did methods of weighing change significantly over the century? How meaningful were annual averages if the number of cattle sold each year varied widely? How competent were the men doing the weighing and, for that matter, how much had they had to drink between weighing the first beast in the morning and the last one towards the end of the day? How accurately and efficiently were weights entered into the ledger? How 'local' were the cattle being sold? Had they come from the hinterland of Cardiff, or been driven from further afield? One could go on. The simple point, of course, is that long runs of data need to be approached with caution and in interpreting such figures we need to know as much as possible of the way in which they have been compiled.

This applies in particular to the Farm Management/Farm Business Survey if it is to be used as a means of illustrating and informing changes in the fortunes of Welsh farming since the mid-1930s. In this context it has to be remembered that the Survey, while modified in various ways over the last 75 years, has

Plate 33. The continuous drive for livestock improvement; T. L. Phillips, Llanboidy exhibits dairy Shorthorn cows at the United Counties Show, 1956

always embraced a *selected* rather than a strictly random sample, contains no part-time holdings and discounts units of less than five acres in size. Besides, it represents only a very small proportion of the total numbers of farms in Wales. The number of holdings annually surveyed may have increased from 350 in 1970 to 550 in 2011, yet the latter figure still only comprises 1.4 per cent of full-time Welsh farms. By the same token, the relative numbers of particular farm types in the sample does not necessarily reflect the prevalence of such farms in the country as a whole. In the 1956–7 sample, for instance, 60 per cent of holdings exceeded 100 acres in size, a far higher proportion than the national figure.

During the past 40 years the size of farms in the Survey sample has virtually doubled and the relative proportions of holdings of different categories have substantially changed. Specialist dairy units, for example, have moved from being less than a quarter of the total sample in the 1960s to around 40 per cent today, with hill and upland sheep and cattle holdings comprising half the sample farms compared with two fifths in the earlier period. The extensive drainage and land reclamation programmes of the 1960s, 1970s and early 1980s may also have had a significant impact on the ratio of 'better land' to 'poor land' farm categories. Effectively, 'better land' farms increased their share of the sample from less than 50 per cent in the early 1960s to almost two thirds by the mid-1980s when the categorisation was abandoned.[1]

Problems of Definition

To complicate matters further, the definitions of the various types of farms included in the Survey sample has also changed with the passing of the years. From the mid-1950s until the early 1980s classification of holdings reflected land quality and elevation and took into account the contribution of rough grazing to the total acreage of each farm. So it was that 'Dairy Farms (Better Land)' yielded more than half their gross output in the form of milk, lay below the 600-foot contour and had little rough grazing. By contrast, 'Dairy Farms (Poor Land)' were located at elevations above 600 feet and had a 'substantial' acreage of rough grazing. Much the same applied to livestock units. Hence 'better land' holdings lay below 1,000 feet and with less than 40 per cent of their acreage comprising rough grazing, relied upon cattle and sheep for the majority of their gross output. Their 'poor land' counterparts were to all intents and purposes hill and mountain farms whose total acreage included more than 50 per cent of rough grazing and whose output primarily involved the sale of store cattle and sheep.

If the use of terms like 'majority' and 'substantial' pose definitional problems, so too does the inherent variability of the 'mixed farm' category, an issue made even more problematic when the 'Dairy Farm (Poor Land)' and 'Mixed Farm (Poor Land)' groups were merged in 1976/7. Like most farms in Britain the great majority of Welsh holdings were 'mixed' when Pryse Howell began his surveys in the 1930s. Of the 60 farms that he studied, *all* had horses and cattle, 96 per cent had sheep and 89 per cent had a few pigs and some farmyard poultry of various descriptions. But the definition of a 'mixed' farm (without, in most cases, the pigs and poultry after the 1960s) remained rather vague and was eventually abandoned in 1982/3 when a wholesale change in categorisation took place in response to the creation of the Less Favoured Areas. This involved classifying farms according to the contribution of specific enterprises to Standard Gross Margin, a procedure leading to the definition of six farm types reflecting sectoral specialisms and location within or beyond a Less Favoured Area. Further changes and sophistications in the mid–1980s resulted in the evolution by 1993/4, of 16 type/size groups which form the basis of the present Survey. Moreover, as ink dries on paper, further imminent changes will witness the demise of the Standard Gross Margin and the birth of the 'Standard Output'.

You Get What you Measure

An earlier chapter discussed the principal objectives of the original Farm Management Survey, which embraced the framing of national policy, the efficiency of individual farms and the conduct of research. Shortly afterwards it was agreed that a fundamental aim of the Survey would be to complement and deepen the teaching of agricultural economics, a function that has benefited many thousands of students over the years. And these students, be they the offspring of farmers or otherwise, learned that the processes and systems used for farm management purposes tend to change with temporal changes in farming itself. Change has also been driven by the penchant for academics, advisors and consultants to develop new ways of doing the same thing, and although this has often proved beneficial, the wood has occasionally been missed for the trees. However, since its inception, the Survey has had the business analysis of the financial performance of the holding at its very heart. As more techniques and instruments have been developed and applied to the farming industry, the format of this analysis has changed, although the original focus has always remained stubbornly clear. Yet merely because the captain knows exactly where and how much water the ship is leaking below the water line, this useful knowledge does not always offer a remedy for saving the vessel. After all, record keeping and analysis, however sophisticated or otherwise, will not necessarily translate into the adoption of best practice and improved production and profitability. Analysis *per se* is of limited diagnostic power at farm or industry level unless used judiciously.

Farm Incomes Over Time

Irrespective of the caveats noted earlier, it would be highly satisfactory if one could trace fluctuations in Welsh farm incomes over the whole period covered by the Survey. Unfortunately, however, Survey results for the later wartime and early postwar years appear to be missing or, at least, available only for short periods or in small samples covering a single enterprise. Thus D.H. Evans's study of 31 dairy farms between 1949–56 reports cash incomes ranging from £456 to £727, while J. Pryse Howell's survey for an earlier period provides rather broader coverage (Table 6).

Table 6. Income per farm on 60 Welsh farms. [2]

Year	Sheep and Cattle (Poor Land)	Sheep and Cattle (Better Land)	Mixed Farms	Cattle and Dairy Farms
1942–3	£312	£304	£428	£576
1941–2	£332	£555	£573	£568
1940–1	£397	£590	£601	£673
1939–40	£183	£386	£431	£512
1938–9	£64	(£8)	£115	£214
1937–8	£198	£93	£135	£297
1936–7	£153	£140	£223	£220

A full and almost continuous run of Farm Management/Business Survey results can be compiled from various sources for most sectors from 1956–7 until the present and these have been used to develop the figures below.[3] Expressing incomes on a per farm, as opposed to a per acre basis has, of course, the obvious drawback in that Net Farm Income might be expected to increase over a period of years as farms get bigger as a result of amalgamations and purchases.[4] On the other hand, farmers, especially in the earlier period, attached a great deal of importance to total farm income and, in any case, net income per farm offers a useful indication of the relative sectoral performance of the industry over a run of years. Whereas this approach allows broad trends to be discerned, year-to-year comparisons are not possible due to annual changes in the composition of the sample. The following figures have been compiled by converting income data to index numbers and deflating these according to living cost changes thereby to provide an assessment of annual real incomes for each sector.[5] Due to problems of shifting definition, data on hill and upland sheep and cattle holdings are not included. In order to resolve the issue of definitional changes within the various other categories, farm types have been combined as follows and are used in Figures 1 and 2 below:

(a) 'Hill and Upland Dairy Farms' and 'Dairy Farms (Poor Land)' ▬

(b) 'Lowland Dairy Farms' and 'Dairy Farms (Better Land)' ▬

(c) 'Hill Sheep Farms' (from 1977–8 only) ──

(d) 'Lowland Cattle and Sheep Farms' and 'Mixed Farming (Better Land)' ▬

(e) Index of Inflation ▬

In each case the index figure represents the annual average of small medium and large farms.

Figure 1:

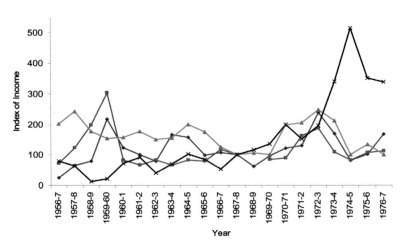

Index of Real Farm Incomes 1956 to 1976
(1967-68 = 100)

Figure 2:

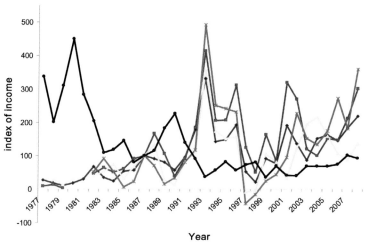

Index of Real Farm Incomes 1977 to 2008
(1987-88 = 100)

This chapter does not pretend to offer an explanatory analysis of changes in the incomes of the various sectors of Welsh farming over the period under review. For any given number of years close reference to the input/output data presented in the Survey is essential to pinpoint specific reasons for short-term temporal changes in sectoral incomes. These technical factors then need to be considered alongside other issues including policy changes and the general situation in the economy as a whole, never forgetting, of course, that omnipresent and all important element, the weather. Some brief interpretative comments are nevertheless offered below by way of illustration of several major trends.

Following the postwar period of growth, the real incomes of the dairy and lowland livestock sectors fluctuated modestly during a period of general economic stability and increasing public prosperity. However, as the 1960s moved on, farmers were confronted by increasing instability along with steadily growing inflationary pressure (Figure 1). Between 1971 and 1973 a favourable combination of good weather, the anticipation of entry into the European Economic Community, rising guaranteed prices, a world shortage of beef and lamb and brucellosis incentive payments for cattle, led to increases in Net Farm Income. The trend was reversed over the next two years as world grain prices pushed up feed costs, fodder was in short supply and store cattle and sheep prices fell in response to world declines. Concurrently, the inflation rate was climbing to alarming levels consonant with the oil crisis arising from conflict in the Middle East. But by 1975/76 cattle and sheep prices had recovered significantly along with both milk yields and prices and, as the price of purchased feeds fell in real terms, so Net Farm Income rose.[6]

As the dangerous inflation of the previous decade was painfully reined in, the British agricultural industry faced a serious cost/price squeeze and farmers' share of agricultural net product declined sharply into the late 1980s (Figure 2). The introduction of milk quotas in April 1984 did little to help the dairy sector which was confronted by escalating costs and although Hill Livestock Compensatory Allowances offered some succour to farmers in Less Favoured Areas, the real incomes of many Welsh livestock producers had dipped to around the level of ten years earlier. Furthermore this took place at a time when the inflation rate was showing worrying signs of increasing once again. Britain's withdrawal from the European Exchange Rate Mechanism in September 1992 yielded a weaker pound and since support payments were fixed in European Currency Units, real returns to farmers in the arable sector tended to increase. Their good fortune, though, was hardly shared by their livestock farming brethren in Wales. While incomes here climbed steeply for a year or so, aided by beef and suckler cow premiums, rising costs prevented any permanent increase in Net Farm Income for either dairy or livestock producers. In the meantime, the traumas of the Bovine Spongiform Encephalitis outbreak in the spring of 1996, with its depressing effects on the beef market, were hardly offset by the introduction of payments under the European Union Agri-Environmental Regulation of some four years previously. On the other hand inflation was once again brought under control and when the miseries of the 2001 epidemic of Foot and Mouth Disease had been overcome, real incomes began to climb, albeit sporadically. Henceforth, subventions under the Single Payment Scheme (introduced in 2003) and environmental payments in various guises would comprise a major, if not *the* major, component of the real incomes of many Welsh farmers.

Flavour of the Month

Information, we are relentlessly told, is power. As agricultural policy became inexorably evidence-based, the establishment of the Farm Management Survey was an attempt to provide more robust evidence of the economic conditions of farming. With the passage of time, consultants enthused over favourite farm management techniques with almost religious conviction, arguing that the use of a particular technique would give the farmer the power to transform a failing business into a successful one. Fees were garnered and expenses docketed and before long consultants moved on to the next 'comparative analysis', 'vertical/proportional analysis' or indeed the now widespread 'benchmarking' catchphrase. But whatever was the fashionable flavour of the month, the Farm Management (and subsequently Farm Business) Survey was, and continues to be, widely recognised as the most authoritative source of accurate information on the financial position of the agricultural industry in Wales and England. With its employment of strict conventions and inbuilt quality guidelines and standards, it was, and remains the watchword for statistical reliability. As methodologies and sampling techniques have changed over time, great care has been taken by the Survey to ensure consistency in all aspects, irrespective of farm type, size or geographical location, while the use of specialised trained personnel to collect the data ensures a high degree of accuracy.

In more recent years, agricultural economics as a discipline within agriculturally based academic institutions has tended to evaporate like the proverbial snowflake in the desert. Whatever the reasons for this decline in a subject area once regarded as fundamentally important by both policy makers and research fund holders, the specialist agricultural economist now ranks among the endangered species. Yet the Farm Business Survey, which in some ways might be viewed as the practical manifestation of generations of progressive refinements in agricultural accounting techniques, remains of foremost importance. The data yielded by the Survey offered an enlightened framework upon which to base policymaking within a national, and later, a European context, while concurrently enabling generations of farmers to make vital management and investment decisions. It continues to do so today and in the future it will play a pivotal role in the evolving needs of an industry whose importance to Wales, Britain and the world can only increase as issues of food security become ever more significant.

Other Possibilities

The database provided by the Survey offers opportunities for detailed quantitative analysis far beyond the crude broad brush observations made earlier in this chapter. Given that both the original *Farm Incomes in Wales* series and the current annual *Statistical Results* publish income and output data for units of different sizes within each farm category, temporal changes in the fortunes of smaller and larger farms might be traced both on a per farm and per acre basis. Equally a more-or-less unbroken run of statistics for almost 60 years permits detailed study of the changing nature of inputs to the various sectors in relation to broader changes in the overall agricultural economy, concurrently allowing for a consideration of the relative contribution of different elements to gross output. How, for example, has the contribution of grants and subsidies in various guises changed as a component of Net Farm Income and Farm Business Income as time has passed? How has the ratio between fertiliser use and purchased concentrate feeds been modified with advances in grassland management practices, and, for that matter, have any discernible changes impacted upon veterinary and medical costs? Temporal variations in labour costs, forage costs, machinery usage (including the role of contractors); these and many other factors of production can be readily determined.

The *Farm Incomes in Wales* publications are restricted to a consideration of farm incomes only. The *Statistical Results*, on the other hand, provide a rather more sophisticated picture with each annual report setting out inter-year comparisons of incomes for identical samples of holdings along with gross margin data per cow and per ewe for the different enterprise types. They include, moreover, aspects of tenants' capital, assets and liabilities and net worth. Over a period of years these sorts of details are likely to be of major importance as a means of tracing changes in capital structure, including land values, building improvements and machinery and livestock investment levels.

Read alongside statistics compiled by the Welsh Assembly Government from the *Survey* data, the annual results of the Farm Business Survey provide a valuable guide to the evolving framework and structure of farming in Wales over a lengthy period, particularly when used in combination with meteorological data and official documentation dealing with changes in farm size, advances in mechanisation, changes in patterns of livestock breeding and other aspects of the farming world.[7] When this data is reviewed in relation to emerging official policy, in particular the broad raft of environmental and welfare legislation of recent decades, the dramatic changes lately confronted by Welsh farming should come sharply into focus. Provided the historian bears in mind the caveats mentioned earlier, the Survey might be seen as a skeleton upon which to drape the flesh of half a century or more of Welsh farming history. What it cannot do, though, is convey any impression of the aspirations, disappointments and even despair of farmers throughout that period of rapid and sometimes traumatic change. This I shall attempt to do in the next chapter.

CHAPTER EIGHT

Continuity and Change

A Disappeared Yet Well Remembered World

THE STEADY GROWTH OF interest in local and regional history over the past half century has spawned an extraordinary output of estate, parish and farming histories based both upon scientifically-conducted sociological studies and upon personal recollections and autobiographical accounts.[1] These works, like many contemporary radio and television programmes, attempt to recapture the atmosphere of a gentler, less distracted and less hurried countryside of the early and middle years of the last century. In physical terms, the broader outlines of that earlier world are still more or less discernible. Meanwhile, some of the details of daily life are recalled by the relict churn stand at the bottom of a farm lane, the old binder abandoned in the corner of some rush-infested field and the horse gear, now scrubbed and polished and proudly displayed on pub wall or over a sitting room fireplace. Besides, there remain today many folk in rude good health who were born and raised in the Welsh countryside around the time when the Farm Management Survey first saw the light of day. Their memories open a window to a world whose relative physical harshness was ameliorated by strong family and community bonds and a profound sense of place and of belonging.

Among their number is Mrs Anne Sherman of Llainmanal,

Rhydlewis, Cardiganshire, born in 1929.[2] The daughter of a Barry schoolmaster, Anne spent all her school holidays at Llainmanal and, in her early teens, passed a complete year on the farm while recovering from pneumonia. She also spent time at Llainmanal while Barry and Swansea coped with the visitations of the Luftwaffe. Featuring in the very earliest years of the Farm Management Survey, Llainmanal was a 45-acre holding belonging to Anne's uncle William George Jones (d. 1948), whose family had long served the Rhydlewis community as teachers, ministers and Overseers of the Poor. Relatively prosperous, the Joneses were perhaps not entirely typical of local small farmers in the 1930s, yet life at Llainmanal remained much as it had been half a century earlier. Domestic electricity was a distant dream, calls of nature were discharged 'down the garden' in the proverbial thunderbox and in the depths of winter water froze in jugs on bedroom dressing tables. Clearly a resourceful girl, Anne managed to avoid this chilly introduction to the day. Managing somehow to get hold of an aluminium hot water bottle, she filled it each evening and by the simple expedient of wrapping it in her underwear and clutching it closely during the night, she was able to enjoy a hot water wash in the morning. For Anne Sherman daily life at Llainmanal remains an enduring part of a kaleidoscope of vivid memories of her childhood and teenage years. (Plate 34) The atavistic smell of farm clothes, of sweat, of animals, and of the soil itself; the fire in the yard and the porcine screams at pig killing time; the busy life of the fields and eventually the 'little grey Fergie' are all indelibly etched on her memory after seven decades. While she played and subsequently worked on the farm, she was expected, as the daughter of professional relatives, to dine apart from the Jones family and their servants. She longed to sit at the old kitchen table to enjoy the banter and chaff of the day, yet she was confined to the parlour and ate from a little table bedecked with a prim white cloth. By this means, argued her bachelor Uncle William, her genteel table manners would not be coarsened by contact with the servants or the less discerning members of the Jones clan.[3]

But come rain or shine, mud or dust, Llainmanal and the countryside around Rhydlewis was a 'little paradise'. So much did she feel intimately bound to this cherished place that the eight-year-old Anne somewhat ghoulishly declared that she wanted her bones to be laid in the Llainmanal farmyard so that the people and animals she had known and loved could walk over her each day. In the event childhood years passed and rites of passage came and went. In 1948 she was taught to drive by the Rhydlewis cobbler/hairdresser/shopkeeper/petrol seller, for which service her father paid the princely sum of £2-10-0 (£2.50). Along with other local girls she watched films at the Rhydlewis YMCA in the early postwar years, paying 6d (2½p) for an evening's entertainment. Returning from her very first 'cinema' visit she was confronted by her Uncle William, a staunch Congregationalist wholly innocent of the film world and its gaudy attractions, with the serious enquiry as to who had been the Chairman!

Plate 34. A demonstration of mechanised ploughing at Llainmanal; William George Jones is towards the centre of the group, his left hand leaning on the plough, c.1914

The cinema and kindred diversions were, of course, out of the question on a Sunday when only the most essential farm tasks were undertaken. As on most farms in rural Wales at the time, the Lord's Day was strictly observed at Llainmanal. Best clothes were worn, chapel or church was dutifully attended and quiet propriety observed for the rest of the day. As Uncle William studiously read the *Farmers Weekly* and his sister Jane put on a fresh apron as she went about her necessary domestic chores, Anne and any other children who happened to be around had to rein in their natural exuberance on this special day.

The contemporary importance of Sunday observance is also emphasised by 74-year-old Mr Hubert Phillips who continues to farm at Llanboidy in Carmarthenshire. (Plate 35) During the early postwar years, recalls Hubert, chapel and church remained vital focal points for local culture and community cohesion, the latter being additionally cemented by close inter-farm cooperation. Neighbours and friends would lend a hand at threshing time and during the potato harvest, with all favours being reciprocated in due course.[4] These group activities, which ultimately served the common good, took place in an atmosphere of bonhomie and good humour, lubricated more often than not with draughts of home brew to keep up the spirits. One Llanboidy farmer, anxious to attract enthusiastic volunteers at times of peak labour demand, added extra sugar to his vat to produce a beer of rare potency. Thirsty locals flocked to the farm gate and laboured until sunset, their exertions fuelled by this heady brew. One imagines that they were kept at arms length from farm machinery, especially where it was on loan from a cooperating neighbour. Either way, cooperative farm work and machinery sharing often gave rise to humorous situations. When Hubert's father borrowed a Bamford hay loader from a neighbour, he found that one of its wheels stubbornly refused to turn. The owner of the machine was perplexed and could only assume that it was being used improperly. "No", observed Phillips senior with a wry smile, "the fact is that you greased one wheel this year and are presumably leaving the other until next year". Hardly side-splitting, perhaps, but nonetheless characteristic of the good-humoured chat among friends, neighbours and relatives who knew each others' fads and foibles and who generally shared common interests and aspirations.

But to return to Llainmanal, which is a working farm no more. In common with many Welsh farms, various family members enjoyed a share in the holding and when Anne Sherman's Uncle William died intestate, a series of complex and costly legal wrangles ensued. As time went by and the lawyers prospered, the property descended to Anne herself, by now married with a family and living in Yorkshire. But like all good Welsh folk she returned to her roots in the 1970s. Selling some land and letting the remainder, she settled in the old house which, though much altered since her childhood and youth, retains its personality and remains the repository of so many happy memories.

Plate 35. Hubert Phillips, Waunfawr, Llanboidy, 2011

The Vanishing Smaller Farm

There are many reasons for families to disappear from farms of which genetic and financial failure are merely two. Children may be indifferent to the land; middle-aged occupiers might not relish the prospect of unremitting hard work later in life; partners might disagree over policy and individuals might be unable to resist the lure of a generous offer from a wealthy neighbour. In these sorts of situations not only does a family bid farewell to a holding which it may have occupied for generations, but in many cases the holding itself disappears from the landscape.

For all the arguments in favour of a progressive 'farming ladder', it is only natural for the go-ahead farmer to want to add acre to acre, thereby to exploit the resultant economies of scale. Whether continually expanding farm size is a *social* good could be argued at length, but the fact of the matter is that since the 1960s and 1970s farms in Wales have increased significantly in size with expansion being officially encouraged and in some ways even enabled by the system of support payments. Together with other factors, including the effects of milk quotas and the decision by the Milk Marketing Board in the 1960s to abandon the milk churn in favour of bulk collection, increasing farm size has inevitably meant a decline in the number of smaller holdings. So too has the ever increasing need for housing and recreation which has swallowed up large numbers of little farms on the urban fringes.

When G.L. Stafford, one of the very last Overseers of the Poor for the village of Crick near Chepstow, returned from active service in the Great War, he was lucky enough to succeed to the tenancy of Bradbury Farm, a holding owned by Monmouthshire County Council. Starting with a milk round and a little market gardening, he eventually developed his 56 acres as a predominantly dairy enterprise, installing the first Alfa Laval milking machine to be seen in Monmouthshire in 1930 and becoming the proud owner of a Ferguson tractor in 1941. Ever resourceful, he promptly adapted his horse drawn machinery to tractor operation. (Plate 36) Stafford continued to work his holding until he retired in 1959, but any hopes which he may have entertained of being succeeded by his sons failed to materialise, since they preferred the infinitely more lucrative careers of medicine and veterinary science. (Plate 37) Accordingly the farm went through a further succession of tenancies until 2006, when the Council made the decision to convert the buildings into dwellings. At present those buildings stand empty and increasingly derelict and, while the farmhouse remains occupied, the land awaits the likely onslaught of bricks and mortar.

Plate 36. G. L. Stafford's son Len, aged 11, riding leading horse at Bradbury Farm, 1935

Plate 37. Len P. Stafford and siblings with their uncle at Bradbury Farm, c.1930

Like Parcmawr Farm near Swansea, which recently disappeared under the weight of 800 houses, Green Yard Farm, one of numerous small dairy farms on the outskirts of Barry, was included in the Farm Management Survey in its early years. Green Yard, however, suffered a rather different fate. During the war years the 43-acre farm supported a small herd of dairy cows linked to a local milk round. It was purchased in 1954 by the father of the present owner, who proceeded to expand the dairy herd by renting extra acres and making full use of the generous grants available in the 1960s and 1970s to upgrade the farm buildings and to install modern parlour and silage facilities. Dairying, however, was abandoned in 1988 and suckled calf production became the mainstay of the business when John Edmunds succeeded his father. His own sons, however, both of whom attended university, showed little taste for life on the land and, after casting about for alternative uses, John developed the place as a golf course, which opened in 1992. (Plate 38)

Plate 38. The original farmhouse at Green Yard Farm, with Mr John Edmunds, 2011

In the mid-1840s the fortunate John Naylor, scion of the Liverpool banking and ship owning family, was given the Leighton Park estate near Welshpool as a wedding present. Consonant with the current fashion for the 'model farm', he spent enormous sums in creating Leighton Farm with its astonishing complex of buildings, covering some 70,000 square feet, and its sophisticated transport systems and waste recycling arrangements.[5] When the estate was broken up in the early twentieth century in order to discharge crippling death duties, the buildings and more than 400 acres of land were purchased by Montgomeryshire (Powys) County Council. At the time there was a great deal of interest in Britain in the idea of land settlement, more especially in providing farms suited to veterans returning from war service who might otherwise find themselves unemployed.[6] With this in mind the Council divided their acquisition into units of approximately 45 acres, of which Gortheur Farm was one. It is not entirely clear whether Gortheur was originally farmed by ex-servicemen, but by the outbreak of the Second World War it was rented by Edgar T. Davies, secretary of the local branch of the National Farmers Union, agent for Unilever and enthusiastic lay preacher. (Plates 39–41) When Davies retired in 1963, the tenancy was taken up by Meurig Mostyn and when he eventually retired in the 1980s, the farm was amalgamated with an adjacent holding. Meanwhile, the complex of Grade II listed Victorian buildings, some of them used for agricultural purposes by Gortheur and other farms and others let for light industrial uses, were beginning to fall into disrepair. To their considerable alarm the Council discovered that in excess of £2 million would be required for their stabilisation and rehabilitation and, being unable or unwilling to shoulder this burden, actively sought a purchaser. For a while nothing happened and the Council's nine tenants continued to farm their acres.

Plate 39. Edgar T. Davies of
Gortheur Farm, Welshpool
and uncle to W. K. Davies

Plate 40. Part of the Leighton model farm complete with Mr W. K. Davies (Garbetts Hall,
Welshpool), 2011

Plate 41. W. E. Davies, father of W. K. Davies, Garbetts Hall

In November 2009, however, the building complex, two hundred acres of land and seven houses were sold to a local businessman who proposes to establish a large equine stud on the site. Like many county council farms elsewhere in Wales, the remaining holdings face an uncertain future.

If some small farms dwindle and disappear, others survive and expand. Tŷ Mawr Farm near Kidwelly comprised 90 acres when it first took part in the Farm Management Survey in the late 1930s. (Plate 42) Small, perhaps by today's standards, but as an arable/dairy farm with an associated milk round, the holding supported six men and thrived under several different owners before it was purchased by John Nixon-Strong in the 1970s. A graduate in agriculture from the University of Reading, he proceeded to double the acreage by absorbing contiguous land and to equip the place with a new range of buildings suited to modern dairy production. The farm continues to prosper today.

It is always as well not to let judgment be coloured by nostalgia and sentimentality. Yet something seems to be lost as small farms disappear, their fields engulfed by a neighbour, manicured into golf courses, planted with caravans or blanketed with houses. Farms, of course, have always been dynamic entities. After all, copyholders of medieval manors in south Wales engrossed their strips in the open field whenever the opportunity arose. Later, prosperous tenant farmers in nineteenth-century Pembrokeshire were not above foreclosing on loans to absorb the holding of a neighbouring small freeholder, while landowners the length and breadth of Wales were quite prepared to add to a tenant's acreage the fields of a neighbour forced by poverty or family circumstances to quit his land. Almost invariably fewer farms and fewer farmers meant (and continues to mean) an ever-diminishing pool of

Plate 42. Tŷ Mawr Farm, Kidwelly, Carmarthenshire

skilled people with an intimate knowledge and understanding of farming and the natural environment at the local level.

In short, as small farms declined in number, the countryside began to empty and the organic rural community started to disintegrate. Anyone doubting this could do worse than to spend a long afternoon walking in the countryside of any part of Wales where ruined houses and tumbledown farmsteads lurk in silent fields, forlorn testimony to an earlier economy. And the silence speaks volumes. Beyond silage making, hay making or harvest, the fields are usually empty of human kind. One might be afforded a glance of a quad bike traversing a distant hill or perhaps of a contractor's JCB gouging its way along a ditch, but as a rule there is little activity in the fields. Sheep and cattle graze below and buzzards and kites float above, but of farming humanity there is usually little sign. A walker might also notice how the face of a lot of farmed land, particularly in the west of the country, has changed over the past generation. As was the case in the 1930s, hedges frequently remain unkempt and bedraggled while bracken, rushes and gorse rampage unchecked and stone walls decay and crumble. How far this dereliction is due to economic factors, shortage of labour (and its crippling cost) or to the rolling out of ill-conceived environmental policies remains an open question. But for all the matchwood timber gates supplied under environmental schemes and for all the well-meaning attempts to create wildlife habitats, the condition of much of today's farmland would be regarded as deplorable by many of those proud and optimistic improvers who took part in the Farm Management Survey in the 1960s and 1970s.

Staying On

The gently-rolling countryside around Llanboidy in Carmarthenshire is ideally suited to grass growing and has long been recognised as a dairy farming area *par excellence*. Indeed, when

Mr Hubert Phillips's father, T.L. Phillips, bought the 118-acre Waunfawr Farm in 1931, virtually all farmers in the area milked cows. (Plate 43) But even then many capital-starved smaller occupiers were turning their backs on farming and selling out to more prosperous neighbours so that the Phillips were eventually able to expand Waunfawr to its present 322 acres. T.L. Phillips had begun to milk-record Welsh Black cows as early as 1927. By the time he retired in 1963, however, he had established a pedigree Shorthorn herd, regularly exhibiting cows at the Carmarthen and Royal Welsh Shows and at the Dairy Show at Olympia. In the meantime, he built a fine new house at Waunfawr and, in 1940, installed a milking machine system within a purpose-built brick cowshed. The machine was powered by a petrol-driven generator which continued in use until 1959 when, following a sustained campaign by the Phillips family to persuade local farmers of its economic worth, the National Grid extended its tentacles to Llanboidy.

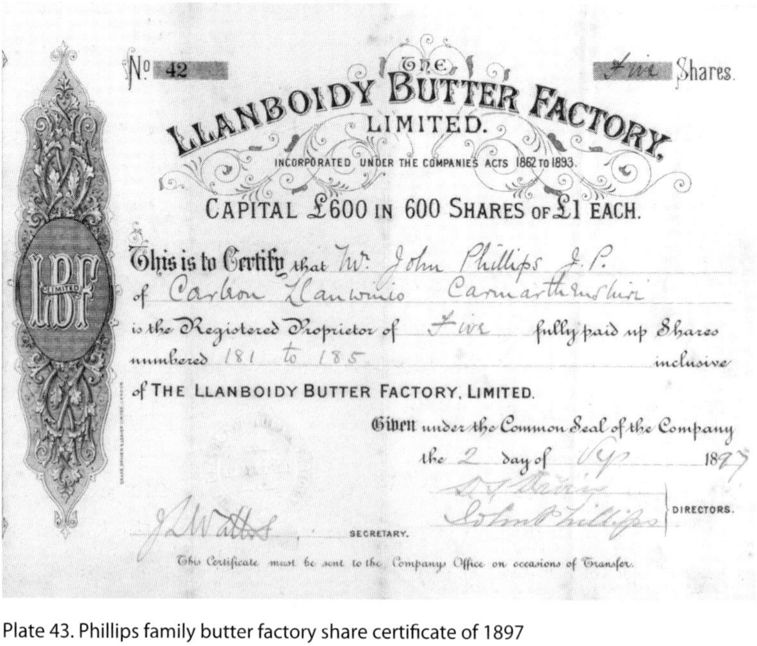

No 42 Five Shares.

THE LLANBOIDY BUTTER FACTORY, LIMITED.

INCORPORATED UNDER THE COMPANIES ACTS 1862 TO 1893.

CAPITAL £600 IN 600 SHARES OF £1 EACH.

This is to Certify that Mr John Phillips J.P. of Carlton Llanwinio Carmarthenshire is the Registered Proprietor of Five fully paid up Shares numbered 181 to 185 inclusive of THE LLANBOIDY BUTTER FACTORY, LIMITED.

Given under the Common Seal of the Company the 2 day of Apr 1897

John Phillips DIRECTORS.

J L Watts SECRETARY.

This Certificate must be sent to the Company's Office on occasions of Transfer.

Plate 43. Phillips family butter factory share certificate of 1897

Throughout the war and during the early postwar years, the Waunfawr cows were paddock grazed in the summer and enjoyed a varied winter diet of kale, rape, mangolds, cabbage and fodder beet, all of it grown on the farm. For a brief period dried grass, processed at a plant near Carmarthen, was included in the ration. But as in other parts of Britain, local enthusiasm for dried grass eventually withered in the face of the sheer effort needed to produce it. Grass had to be cut, turned, swathed and loaded onto an ex-army lorry with a green crop loader, for transport to Carmarthen where it was dried, baled and eventually returned. An excellent product, no doubt, but one which was expensive to produce and cumbersome to feed. Besides, following Phillips's wartime trials with oat and vetch silage conserved in a circular silo, silage had now come to form the bulk of the winter diet for the cows at Waunfawr.

As the war came to an end and the resident land girl from Cardiff went tearfully home and the prisoners-of-war who had drained the lower meadows of Waunfawr returned to an uncertain future in Europe, T.L. Phillips bought his first tractor. Ten years old at the time, Hubert Phillips recalls his intense excitement and fascination as the new David Brown, complete with trailer and side rake, was delivered from Carmarthen. His experience probably mirrored that of many a Welsh farmer's lad in the late 1940s and 1950s as farm mechanisation haltingly penetrated the far-flung corners of the country.

When Hubert Phillips completed his studies at Pibwrlwyd Agricultural College the postwar drive for production and efficiency was getting into full swing. He took over from his father in 1963 and immediately set about effecting change by purchasing Dairy Friesian heifers and 'grading up' the Shorthorn herd with Friesian bulls.[7] Concurrently, he exploited the full range of government subsidies and grants as he installed cubicle housing and extensive silage storage facilities and made improvements to existing buildings. As time went by, silage came to form the entire winter bulk feed for the herd which, by the early 1970s, was being milked in an 8:8 herringbone parlour equipped with electronic feeders to dispense bought-in concentrates. This was replaced by a 12:12 unit in 1984, shortly after additional quota had been purchased. Hubert Phillips continued to preside over extraordinary developments at Waunfawr. Fields were drained, new roads were constructed, sophisticated buildings were erected and an automated scraper and slurry disposal system installed, thereby allowing the herd to expand from 30 cows in the 1960s to 160 in 2005.

Ironically, just as the farm approached the peak of its productivity and efficiency, nature intervened. Badgers had always been seen in the locality, but by the early 2000s they were becoming almost pestilential and as their numbers increased so tuberculosis became a serious problem at Waunfawr. After several difficult and worrying years, the herd was finally declared free of the disease and Hubert Phillips decided that now, perhaps, was the time to discontinue dairying.[8] As the pressure of the years began to build, less, rather than more worry was the order of the day, and the Waunfawr herd was sold in September 2005.

But silence descended only temporarily on the farmstead and Hubert remains very much in harness. He now lets out 200 acres of Waunfawr each summer, taking two crops of silage from the rest of the land which sustains 250 cattle of various descriptions overwintered in the buildings on behalf of other farmers. So it is that the farm remains a vibrant and viable unit under Hubert Phillips's direction and will continue as such until he is succeeded by his son, a London-based businessman. The latter may well want to run things rather differently to his father, but whatever the future may bring Waunfawr stands as a fine example of the rewards to be earned from land well-farmed by thoughtful and creative farmers.

Adjusting to Circumstances

Originally the seat of the old Welsh Blayney family, Aberbechan near Newtown was purchased from the Gregynog estate by the grandfather of the present owner in the year before the outbreak of the Great War. (Plate 44) Standing prominently on the eastern side of a charmingly wooded valley running up to Bettws Cedewain, the farm supports a fine timber-framed house. This may well occupy the site of the *plas* of Owen of Aberbechan, a man of singular attributes described in the sixteenth century by Lewis Glyn Cothi as being like a swan "… as white as a water lily from Tregynon yonder".[9]

When John Price's grandfather bought the place, it embraced 150 acres along with 30 acres of semi-derelict woodland. Run as a beef and sheep farm in the 1930s, almost half the acreage was ploughed in response to official requirements during the Second World War, some of it with the help of prisoners-of-war from the camp at Mochdre several miles distant.[10] In due course, John Price's father inherited the farm and young Price was despatched

Plate 44. Aberbechan, Newtown, 2011

to Llysfasi Agricultural College. It is probably true to say that the extramural interests of agricultural students tend on the whole to be of the bucolic and sporting rather than the reflective and artistic varieties. To this generalisation, John was a singular exception, being a cellist of no mean ability who performed with the National Youth Orchestra of Wales and who continues at present to play a prominent role in local musical circles.

If music and musical performance was a major focus, John joined his father on the farm in the mid-1960s, setting up a 20 sow pig herd to provide himself with some independence of income. Selling weaners to the Wynnstay Weaner Group proved satisfactory for a while, but after the 1967 Foot and Mouth Disease outbreak, when movement restrictions forced him to retain large numbers of pigs at home, profits began to decline and the enterprise was eventually abandoned.

Henceforth effort has been concentrated on finished lamb and store cattle production, presently against a background of involvement in the *Tir Gofal* scheme. Additionally, the farm carries an important supplementary enterprise developed in collaboration with *Coed Cymru*. This originally involved nothing less than the wholesale rehabilitation of the 30 original acres of farm woodland along with a further 30 acres purchased in 2000. By way of a range of management practices, aimed both at creating a valuable income stream and at enhancing local wildlife habitats, the woodlands now produce valuable timber for furniture making, building and fuel. In other words, they have reverted to their original function which had begun to lapse in the early nineteenth century when so many Welsh woodlands were overexploited for ship building and industrial uses. The magnificence of the timber-framed houses and weather-boarded outbuildings of many mid-Montgomeryshire farms bears witness to the former importance of local oak plantings and, in a sense, John has paid homage to previous generations of craftsmen by personally fashioning new doors for the Aberbechan house from the oaks of his own woodlands. His handmade oak chairs, moreover, together with sales of manufactured wood products and dressed timber, contribute significantly to overall farm income.

John Price derives great pleasure from his forestry work and it is a tribute to his enterprise and enthusiasm that forestry students from Bangor University are regular visitors to the Aberbechan woods, which also play host to parties of pupils from local schools.[11]

In the years ahead John, now 63, proposes to concentrate his efforts on the woodland side of the business while his son, a physics graduate working in local industry, will manage the farm on a 'dog and stick' basis. Thus will the national capital be protected and improved. As dynamic management yields productive woodland, so the agricultural land will remain in good heart to await the inevitable day when the politicians in charge of a grossly overpopulated island awake to the vital importance of once again producing food from our own resources. (Plate 45)

Plate 45. John Price, Aberbechan, Newtown, 2011

Confronting the Future

Just as every farm and every farmer is unique, so the issue of generational succession varies according to myriad individual circumstances. Succession is normally a straightforward enough matter when one or more offspring are enthusiastic for the land and appreciative of its capacity to provide them with a fulfilling way of life. But indifference to the land and even active dislike for farming on the part of the next generation can pose problems and lead to sleepless nights for many a farmer.

Tŷ Ucha'r Llyn at Gwyddelwern near Corwen stands between 750 and 1,000 feet above sea level facing the Clocaenog Forest to the north-west, with the Dee Valley and the Berwyns to the south. Dylan Parry is the third generation of his family to own the 140-acre holding which he farms along with a further 110 rented acres. (Plate 46) As the diaries of Dylan's grandfather and father reveal, the farm was much improved from the 1950s into the 1970s. Throughout this period, dairying had been the principal enterprise, but when confronted with the need to find substantial capital sums to modernise buildings and equipment, the Parrys took the decision to move away from milking in favour of developing a beef and sheep enterprise. This is currently based upon the sale of finished lambs, store cattle and suckler cows with calves at foot, the latter being produced from purchased bulling heifers.

While Mrs Parry works full-time away from the farm, her husband supplements the family income by cutting grass on a contract basis for schools local to the Ruthin/Bala area. These several sources of funds contribute to the support both of the Parrys and their four children (of whom the two eldest sons are 23 and 21 respectively and both in employment) and Dylan's retired parents who live nearby.

Apart from the day-to-day business of running the farm and household and of sustaining non-farming jobs and activities, the

Plate 46. The Parrys of Tŷ Ucha'r Llyn, Gwyddelwern, Corwen, 2011

Parrys wrestle with the question of accommodating the next generation. Their eldest son presently works in the building trade although, quite understandably, his parents would like to encourage him to return to full-time work on the farm. But what incentive would there be for a young man to give up a decently paid and stress-free trade for the uncertainties and worries of farm life? In the twenty-first century appeals to the simple codes of loyalty and the imperative of maintaining family continuity have a habit of falling onto barren ground. Yet, the idea of an increased and sustainable farm income might give pause for thought and the Parrys are examining a number of possibilities. There is some potential to expand the grass cutting operation (although it could be argued that this might be to the detriment to the daily management of the farm), but further development of the beef and sheep enterprise is limited by acreage. On the face of it options seem limited, although the elevation of the farm hints at the possibility of wind farming as a solution. After all, to paraphrase Mrs Parry, since one cannot avoid seeing a neighbour's flourishing crop of turbines from the farmyard, why not turn over part of the holding to their use? The idea would be to view wind farming as a capital-generating venture by which the family could accumulate the wherewithal to purchase more land. (Plate 47) Acquisition of more acres would in turn create the potential for boosting farm income to a level which might encourage the eldest son to return to his heritage.

At first glance this might seem a perfectly reasonable proposal. But, as Dylan ruefully observes, the local land market is complicated by emotional and sentimental considerations arising from close blood relationships between farming families in the immediate area. A neighbouring rented farm may come up for sale, but if this is occupied by a relative, however distant, issues of kinship, custom and manners may influence a decision whether or not to bid for the land. This seems to hark back to a much

Plate 47. A potential solution? Wind turbines within view of Tŷ Ucha'r Llyn

earlier and noble Welsh tradition where loyalty to clan and kith and kin overrode economic considerations and the dictates of 'the market'.[12] In any event it demonstrates the extraordinary complexities and nuances of the land market and the non-economic considerations involved in parts of the country where many families have lived for generations. It also highlights just one of the conundrums faced by progressive farmers wishing to expand their businesses and to ensure generational continuity.

Some Pressures and Constraints

To a ghostly visitor from 1936, the physical appearance of most of the Welsh countryside would be more or less recognisable. There is more softwood timber in the hills than three quarters of a century ago, more black and white cattle on the lowland pastures, more concrete and asbestos in the steading and more bungalows in the villages, yet the broader features of the country remain much as they were. The most profound difference, and this would strike our visitor most forcefully, rests in the nature of the rural community itself.

Irrespective of depopulation and associated demographic problems, rural Wales between the wars still retained at least some vestiges of a centuries-old tradition of community cooperation. Competition for prizes at *eisteddfodau* and other cultural events was fiercely fought. But when it came to the all-important business of the land itself, cooperation in pursuit of the common good had a habit of overriding individual interests. Meanwhile a sense of place and deep-rootedness seemed to many people adequate compensation for lack of amenities and opportunities for advancement. Those who resisted the temptation to migrate to the industrial valleys of the south, or to the cities and towns of England, remained in their villages, hamlets and farmsteads and nurtured a system of core values which lay great emphasis on community cohesion.

This has now all but disappeared. There are, of course, plenty of cases of inter-farm cooperation where no money changes hands, but the earlier notion of farm/cottage community interdependence has evaporated as rural properties have been acquired by outsiders with no farming background or local loyalties. Few would doubt the economic benefits accruing to outsider investment, yet there are many who have serious reservations on both cultural and demographic grounds. Either way, as workers continue to leave the farms and rural homes cease to have any organic connection with the land around them, the countryside has turned into a rather lonely place for those in whose stewardship it remains.

For the man who milks dairy cows twice daily for 350 days each year, or who manages a remote upland sheep holding, farming is becoming an increasingly solitary occupation. Long hours, isolation, stress and restricted opportunities for social contact sometimes make it difficult for younger farmers to find wives or partners, while there are strong indications that farmer divorce rates are higher than those of the general population.[13] Moreover, academic studies of the 719 farmer suicides in Wales and England between 1981 and 1993 and more recent analyses of stresses within the farming community reveal considerably higher levels of depression and suicidal tendencies among farmers than among other occupational groups.[14]

Given these sobering facts, most people would probably agree that practical and emotional support would be welcomed by the great majority of farmers running businesses which are so often 'one-man shows'. Yet financial pressures, social changes and the perceived need for a degree of independence and contact with a world away from farming has meant that, in more recent years, spouses and partners have sought jobs and social lives beyond the home farm. Many, like Dylan Parry of Gwyddelwern, take the view that in the present challenging times, an off-farm income is an essential ingredient of survival. Others, however, facing up to the daily demands of more complex businesses, attach a great deal of value to the support of a partner who chooses to remain at home.

Gwyn Jones farms 300 acres in coastal Cardiganshire in partnership with his wife Enid, son Gareth and father-in-law David Morgan. The farm presently carries 500 sheep, 200 beef cattle and a large and fully appointed caravan site which, at the height of the season, caters for upwards of a thousand visitors at any one time. (Plate 48) As the site has become an increasingly prominent contributor to family income, so farming practices have been modified. 'Site pressures' contributed to the eventual demise of a large dairy herd, while early lambing has been adopted to ensure that the bulk of the work with the sheep flock is completed before the summer vacation season. In essence, the farming side of the business has been adapted to fit in with the demands of a sophisticated holiday site. Gwyn pays fulsome tribute to his wife's support. Without her input in running the site shop, organising bookings and dealing with business accounts, to say nothing of managing the family home, his task would be difficult, if not impossible. This raises the more general point that while a partner's work outside the farm may make a useful (and sometimes essential) contribution to household income, there are inevitable downside effects. After all, beyond any direct role they may play in the business, a partner's daily physical presence offers the opportunity for emotional and psychological support when things may be going awry. The strains of a long spell of inclement weather, the *angst* of an outbreak of livestock disease or even an uncharitable letter from the bank can at least be eased when there is a sympathetic shoulder to lean upon and a willing ear to listen. This sort of support might seem all the more important when the farm is located in some remote spot far from sound and view of neighbours.

Plate 48. General view of Morfa, Llanrhystud, Cardiganshire, 2011

Living with Nature

It might be supposed that the juxtaposition of a holiday site with a working farm would help to bring a least some people into closer contact with the sources of their food. The old belief claimed by many country folk, that urban dwellers tend to be wholly ignorant of the origin of the food on their plates, has passed from myth to reality with the alarming realisation that many visitors to supermarkets have no concept of the working of farm systems or of the conditions under which food is produced. This may, in part, be the fault of the industry and the inability of its representatives to articulate the farming case and to underline the absolute importance of food production in the context of the broader countryside debate. Somehow, it seems that when rural matters are discussed in the media, the voice of farming itself seems muted, hesitant and even apologetic. Officialdom, meanwhile, has a craven habit of succumbing to what is often less than enlightened public opinion when it comes to countryside issues.

Nowhere is this more the case than in the matter of wildlife and environmental conservation. Apart from those few remaining monoculturalists, who regard their activities as little more than a business, farmers are only too aware of the link between the prosperity of a well-run farm and the wellbeing of the wildlife resident upon it. Dylan Parry of Gwyddelwern was born and bred to the land and, having learned as a boy of the need to protect natural habitats, actively attempts to promote wildlife on his farm. Dylan argues that since he knows every square foot of his land, he is probably the best judge of how to farm its acres to the mutual benefit of his family and the wild creatures sharing it with him. What sticks in his craw is the incessant flow of advice and direction emanating from 'experts' with little knowledge of local conditions. Reflecting on the changes in farming over recent decades, he mirrors the views of many farmers in expressing his resentment of the off-farm pressures imposed by the demands of environmental management, to say nothing of the baleful hand of 'health and safety'. Aware of the taxpayer's right to call at least some notes of the rural tune, Dylan is equally aware of the abiding virtue of common sense.

Dylan Parry's opinion is shared by dairy and sheep farmer John ap Hywel of Garnfach near Llanrhystud in Cardiganshire.[15] He maintains that any decent farmer "worth his salt" will be, almost by definition, an environmentalist. At the same time he deplores the "rural slums" created by a countryside management policy that encourages drains to be blocked to generate bogs and promotes the virtual abandonment of productive land and its reversion in many cases to semi-scrub of limited environmental or amenity value. Like Gwyn Jones, he would argue that while farming and conservation need to proceed hand-in-hand, the national interest is best served when productive land is allowed to produce. Both men view with alarm the negative public attitudes towards farming stirred up by those termed by John "the urban chattering classes". But, in the face of a generally hostile media, which has failed to show how commercial pressures and the supermarket stranglehold has forced many farmers into courses of action which they might otherwise have avoided, Gwyn concludes stoically that he and his fellows have little alternative but to "revert to type and quietly get on with it". Barri Williams, who farms sheep, sucklers and store cattle near Tregaron, agrees. But what a strange "Alice in Wonderland world it is," he muses, "when millions of pounds of taxpayers' money is spent by one generation in drainage, reclamation and upland improvement, only to be squandered by a later generation in creating wilderness!"

These three men, wholly different in their political perspectives and academic backgrounds are at one in their belief that farming is essential in maintaining the traditional pattern of the Welsh landscape so beloved of tourists and travellers, poets and artists.[16] Perhaps even more important, hints Barri, is the need to maintain a vibrant farming base in Wales against a future time when "it will become more difficult to balance food production and conservation".

Then and Now

From the standpoint of public perception, the history of Welsh farming highlights several intriguing parallels between the situation in 1936 when Farm Management Survey investigators first began to stalk the countryside and that prevailing in 2011. The overall position at the end of the 'dark decade' was summed up by the commentator and polemicist Malcolm Muggeridge in typically laconic fashion:

> If the Preservation of Rural England was a cause which attracted
> adherents and sometimes money, the Productivity of Rural England
> aroused little concern. The Ministry of Agriculture was the grave
> of the political expectations of its successive occupants. Quotas and

bounties and, later, marketing schemes, would not make the soil increase its yield. The harvest was largely pensionable officials, of these a fine crop.[17]

Although the agricultural workforce still comprised 6.7 per cent of the total UK workforce in 1936, farming was nevertheless seen to be of little more than marginal importance by a population enjoying seemingly inexhaustible supplies of cheap imported food. Yet there was a widely-held belief in academic circles (which eventually found expression in the 1942 Scott Report on land utilisation) that progressive rural decline could only be arrested by the creation of a prosperous, science-based agricultural industry. As agricultural pundits and propagandists argued the case, a few lone voices, notably from among members of the Society for the Protection of Natural Resources, quietly suggested that a modern, technology-driven farming world would have negative implications for wildlife. But on the whole this was studiously ignored, especially by the Ministry of Agriculture, which for decades remained totally aloof from matters of environmental or wildlife conservation.

In the meantime the hustle and bustle of town life went on and to the consternation of public health officials, the overcrowding and squalor of many Victorian tenements and closely-packed terraces was as bad, if not worse, than a generation previously. As towns became noisier and dirtier, leading to the founding of the Anti-Noise League, the Noise Abatement Society and the Anti-Litter League among other well-meaning bodies, the countryside came to be seen as a haven of relief. It might be populated with bumpkins, yokels, dangerous dogs and bulls, yet its air was fresh and clear and its tracks and lanes safe to roam. Even before the 1938 Holidays-with-Pay Act, youth and cycling organisations had arranged weekend jaunts in the country, while less active working folk flooded into the countryside on charabanc trips arranged by their factory and office employers. And, to the great dismay of protectionist bodies, car ownership began inexorably to spread to the lower-middle and even working classes. In 1919 around 100,000 motors chugged their way around Britain, but within 20 years car numbers had expanded to 2.3 millions bringing in their wake the inevitable petrol stations, garages and cheap roadhouses which raised the collective blood pressure of contemporary ruralist writers.

The descent of the urban hordes occasioned much moaning and gnashing of teeth. That they left behind their rubbish and picnic leftovers was bad enough, but of far greater concern was the potential effect on the sturdy respectability of country folk of contact with flashy and meretricious townspeople! Countryside propagandists postulated a future wherein the solid rural 'virtues' (however mythical!) were lost as the countryside became urbanised. (Plate 49) This was very much the viewpoint of the Council for the Preservation of Rural Wales (CPRW), founded in 1928 "to prevent the spoliation and necessary destruction" of rural Wales by unplanned development, urbanisation and visitor pressure. The CPRW, a rather gentrified body, was given tacit support by Plaid Cymru, whose earlier luminaries adopted an anti-urban and anti-industrial philosophy, believing that a return to rural roots was an essential element in nation-building. It is difficult to avoid the conclusion that the CPRW, like its English equivalent, was established to protect the countryside for those lucky enough to live in it. The organisation certainly crossed swords with several leftwards leaning bodies. The Ramblers Association, for example, looked upon the CPRW as a reactionary and conservative clique quite incapable of realising that sensible development in rural Wales would not necessarily clash with countryside interests.[18]

Almost a century and an apocalyptic war later, the CPRW and the Ramblers Association continued to contribute to the rural debate in Wales. But they did so against a very different background. Once the experience of war had emphasised the importance of a thriving agricultural sector, any discussion of environmental and wildlife issues or of matters relating to amenity or access to the countryside could not ignore the realities of daily farming life. Or at least, so it seemed to most reasonable people. On balance, legislative measures taken between the 1970s and 1990s to protect wildlife habitats, historic landscapes and the archaeological heritage took careful note of the needs of farming in its various guises. At the same time, facilities for visitors to the Welsh countryside improved, while the more discerning among the visitors themselves began to take interest in the farming world around them.

Plate 49. A gentler and less distracted age; a mare suckles her foal at Aberbechan, Newtown, c.1935

New Concerns

More recently the atmosphere has changed. To public worries over the potential effects of agrochemicals and developments in molecular biology on the environment and the food chain has been added a deep and growing concern about modes of animal production and domestic animal health and welfare. This has been variously manifest in polemical campaigns in the press, in television and radio features and in threats and acts of violence against individuals. How far these public concerns are justifiable or are merely the well-orchestrated exaggerations of a small, but articulate animal welfare lobby is not the business of this chapter. My business is the condition of farms and farming.

In preparing this book I have spoken to many farmers whom I had not previously met and to others who have been friends and neighbours for some years. It would be pleasant to record the conclusion that the present-day farmscape of Wales rests under the stewardship of a group of contented and fulfilled people confident in the future prosperity of their industry. It would, at the same time, be wholly inaccurate to do so. Farmers in Wales are frustrated, over-regulated and angry. While appreciative of many of the benefits of EC membership, they feel let down by successive governments in thrall to what they see as irritating, unnecessary and counterproductive edicts emanating from Brussels. But above all, Welsh farmers feel bemused and beleaguered by what they perceive as a lack of public understanding of their trade.

On the whole those farmers who joined the Farm Management Survey in 1936 were undercapitalised and operated with a tool kit which had hardly advanced in 20 years. Besides, with the notable exception of milk producers most traded in a wholly unprotected market in competition with cheap imports from the Empire and elsewhere. Yet visitors to Wales could hardly help noticing that farming, even if it was little more than the 'dog and stick' variety, was the very focus and fulcrum of countryside activities. Farming supported local trades, it provided (albeit at an ever-diminishing rate) employment for local people, it gave business to wheelwrights, blacksmiths, coopers, hurdle makers, hedgers and ditchers and other specialist craftsmen. In other words, farming, even at a time of agricultural depression, was pivotal to the economic and social fabric of rural Wales.

But however much one might wish it otherwise, the farm is no longer the epicentre of the rural world. Providing food is deemed by officialdom to be merely part of a complex of countryside functions and there are even those who would argue in favour of affording conservation and amenity issues priority over agriculture in the management of the Welsh landscape. So it is that many farmers in twenty-first century Wales, although for the most part enjoying relative prosperity and financial comfort, feel marginalised and even vilified.

A Crossroads

In a sense, today's Welsh farmer approaches a rather similar crossroads to that encountered by his grandfather in 1939 when, after a generation of semi-neglect, farms were called upon to support an industrial nation faced with the very real prospect of total blockade and starvation. Seventy-five years on and the world remains an unstable place, while the combined effects of climate change and population growth have forced the issue of food security to the forefront of debate. A few years ago, before the shifting sands of the international financial world revealed the folly of over-reliance on 'service' industries, talk of self-sufficiency and of producing more food from our own resources as a means of import saving was hardly taken seriously. If the era of structural surpluses had passed, the booming economy at home meant that the country could easily afford to cover the cost of imported foods. This, in turn, meant that home food production needed no longer to take absolute priority when it came to the overall management of the countryside. But in a very short space of time, the situation has dramatically changed and in the second decade of the twenty-first century the importance of food miles and home production is once again being emphasised in official circles. It may well be that by the time the Farm Management/ Business Survey celebrates its centenary, Welsh producers and their colleagues eastwards of Offa's Dyke will once again be exhorted to maximise food production from every single acre. We can only hope that in the meantime as much of our land as possible remains farmable, that farming skills remain abundant, and that public indifference and obloquy does not entirely crush the enthusiasm of farmers for their calling.

POSTSCRIPT

THE BRAVE ATTEMPTS ON the part of a number of far-sighted Welshmen to raise funds for a Welsh university gained momentum in the 1860s as "the aggregated pittances of humble people" began to accumulate.[1] For more than a century after its foundation in 1872, the University College of Wales at Aberystwyth repaid the faith and trust of the little people whose sixpences and half-crowns had been so vital in the early years by offering all manner of extramural educational opportunities within the community. Peripatetic agricultural lecturers explained the mysteries of manuring in church and chapel halls, well-scrubbed instructresses emerged from the dairies in the basement of the Old College to travel the countryside demonstrating the principles of clean milk production, while some of their female colleagues instructed local folk in the arcane arts of poultry dressing. But bucolic practical instruction was only a small part of extramural outreach. The University despatched lecturers around the countryside to teach languages, politics, international affairs, local history and, indeed, virtually any subject for which there was reasonable local demand. The University, in effect, was an integral element in the educational framework of the more general community and remained so for many years.

In its earliest years, the Farm Management Survey formed part of this framework. Although the Survey was conceived first and foremost as a means of monitoring of the farming industry, its officers gave advice and encouragement to farmer collaborators. In so doing, it could be argued that they played an important role in breaking down the traditional distrust of farmers for 'figures' and

175

their reluctance to engage in discussion of their financial affairs. As the annual reports of the Survey were published and carefully studied by farmers throughout the country, the realisation that economic management was every bit as important as technical competence began to dawn. Survey data highlighted elements of inefficiency, underlined weak aspects of management and suggested potential areas of enterprise expansion or contraction.

As the Survey developed, so did the farming world. Increasingly sophisticated methods of analysis allowed for increasingly sophisticated and detailed investigations of the economics of different farming systems and enterprises. As computer technology developed, the work of investigational officers changed and some of the more complex decision making at farm level was facilitated. Meanwhile the data collected from farmer clients served not only to contribute to the bank of information gathered by the authorities as an aid to policy making, but was, and remains, a vital element in the teaching of farm business management and economics at Aberystwyth.

Irrespective of three-quarters of a century of change and development, officers working within the Survey continue to nurture and cherish the close relationship with their collaborating farmers. After 75 years the Survey continues to be held in high regard by the Welsh farming community and for many farmers it represents a continuation of the principle of outreach avidly pursued by the University more than a century ago. In addition, the continued location of the Survey within a major Department of the University indicates the significance attached by the institution to the profound importance of farming in Welsh life.

Farming has moved a long way in 75 years. Few of the original farmers who took part in the early years of the Survey could have imagined such extraordinary developments as round-the-clock milking, satellite-aided crop management and genetic modification. Underpinned by government and commercially-funded scientific research, farming has now become a much more precise business than was the case in the late 1930s. Animal management, the concern of most Welsh farmers, has been made the easier by great swathes of research in the field of animal health which have provided opportunities for curing, or at least controlling, pathological conditions which were fatal two generations ago. In addition, advances in nutritional understanding and housing requirements have facilitated standards of animal welfare far in advance of those of the pre-war period. After all, increasing intensification in some sectors of the animal production industry has been paralleled by quantum increases in our knowledge of animal behaviour which in turn has led to the development of strict codes of husbandry practice designed to ensure a decent quality of life for the animals upon which most of us depend.

But if the management of livestock has become more 'scientific' (or less hit-and-miss) than in earlier times, it is still in large measure an art. The capacity for detailed observation, a deep well of patience, intuition and empathy are all qualities required by the good animal husbandman. And these qualities are demanded in equal measure when it comes to the management and stewardship of the land.

As I have mentioned elsewhere in this book, the land of Wales, like the land of other nations within our islands, is the *only* genuine national capital. To neglect that land or to manage it without regard for the future or for the common good is tantamount to treason. Our farmers *created* the agricultural landscape more than five millennia ago and have been developing it along productive lines ever since. As surveys undertaken in two twentieth-century world wars make abundantly clear, farming has helped to save our culture and way of life from extinction on at least two occasions. More recently, though, the Farm Business Survey has shown the willingness with which the Welsh farming community has come to terms not only with environmental and wildlife habitat issues, but with the public's desire for greater access to the countryside. As we celebrate three quarters of a century of the Welsh Farm Business Survey and Welsh farming we can only hope that over the years ahead the natural environment will continue to be respected *and* that our land will be sustainably managed with a view to producing food for an overcrowded island.

Appendix I

Senior Management of the Farm Management/Business Survey, 1936–2011

1936–46

A.W. Ashby, MA, CBE, Professor of Agricultural Economics, Provincial Agricultural Economist and Director of the Farm Management Survey.

1946–62

E.F. Nash, MA, Professor of Agricultural Economics, Provincial Agricultural Economist and Director of the Farm Management Survey. (Between 1936–52 J. Pryse Howell, MA served as Assistant Advisor and subsequently Independent Lecturer and undertook day-to-day Survey management.)

1963–4

D.H. Evans, BA and J.R.E. Phillips BA, MA jointly oversaw the Survey pending a professorial appointment.

1964–76

H.T. Williams, MA, CBE, F.R.Agric. Soc, Professor of Agricultural Economics, Provincial Agricultural Economist and Director of the Farm Management Survey. (W. Dyfri Jones, MSc, undertook day-to-day management between 1968–78.)

1976–94

D.I. Bateman MA, Professor of Agricultural Economics.

Bateman was uneasy with the notion of Wales as a 'province' and was content to allow the title of 'Provincial Agricultural Economist' to fall into abeyance. Under his Departmental headship the direction of the Farm Management (and subsequently Business) Survey devolved as follows:

1978–88

D.A.G. Green, BSc, PhD, Senior Lecturer in Agricultural Economics.

1988–2003

T.N. Jenkins, BSc, PhD, Senior Research Associate in Agricultural Economics. Upon Bateman's retirement Peter Midmore was appointed as a replacement, but the latter was soon redeployed to the School of Management and Business as Professor of Applied Economics. The Chair in Agricultural Economics at Aberystwyth, the first to be established in Britain, no longer exists. The Farm Business Survey, however, continues to flourish.

2003–Present

A. O'Regan, BSc, MBA, Lecturer in Rural Business Management.

Appendix II

Current Staff of the Farm Business Survey (Plate 50)

Director: A. O'Regan, BSc, MBA

Computer Officer: N.D.H. Chapman, BSc, MSc

Senior Investigational Officers
R.R.G. Davies, ARAgS CDA; N.C. Reeves, BSc; D.H. Williams, BSc;
I.R. Williams, BSc; T.W. Roberts, ND, BSc

Investigational Officers
A. Davies, BSc, MSc, PhD, Dip.Ed.; W. Morris, BSc, MSc;
D.E. Jones, HND, BSc; E.R. Jones, HND

Clerical Assistants
J.E. Edwards; B. Jones

Plate 50. FBS staff employed during the anniversary year.
From left. Standing: Nick Reeves, Ian Williams, Huw Williams, Nigel Chapman, Rowland Davies, Dylan Jones and Wyn Morris. Seated: Eileen Edwards, Tegid Roberts, Tony O'Regan (Director), Eric Jones and Brenda Jones.

Notes

Chapter 1

[1] P. Reid, *The Dark Valley; A Panorama of the Nineteen Thirties* (London, 2000).

[2] Labour at this time was committed to a policy of land nationalisation, only to abandon this after 1945 on the grounds both of cost and hopeless impracticability. (M. Titchelar, 'The Labour Party and the retreat from rural land nationalisation during the Second World War', *Agricultural History Review*, 51, 2003, pp.209–225.

[3] T. Rooth, 'Trade Agreements and the Evolution of British Agricultural Policies in the Nineteen Thirties', *Agricultural History Review*, 35, 1985, p.190.

[4] Improvements in arterial drainage set the scene for the enormous expansion of tile drainage in the early postwar years. Drainage of the lowlands of Wales and England was a major factor in the growth of agricultural productivity during that period. (J. Bowers, 'Inter-War land drainage and policy in England and Wales', *Agricultural History Review*, 46, 1998, pp.64–80.

[5] P. Brassley, J. Burchardt and L. Thompson, *The English Countryside between the wars; Regeneration or Decline?* (Woodbridge, 2006), p.235.

[6] See, for example, D.W. Howell, *Land and People in Nineteenth Century Wales* (London, 1977), *passim*.

[7] J. Saville, *Rural Depopulation in England and Wales, 1851–1951* (London, 1957).

[8] A.W. Ashby and J.M. Jones, 'The Social Origin of Welsh Farmers', *Welsh Journal of Agriculture*, 2, 1926, p.19.

[9] R.G. Stapledon, *The Land Now and Tomorrow* (London, Faber, 1935). For the period in general see, R.J. Moore-Colyer, 'Farming in Depression; Wales between the wars, 1919–1939,' *Agricultural History Review*, 46, 1998, pp.177–196.

[10] Since its foundation in 1872, the College at Aberystwyth has had several different names, having finally (?) settled for 'Aberystwyth University'. I shall refer to it as 'the University' throughout the rest of this book.

[11] J.M. Jones, 'Welsh Agriculture in transition', *Agriculture*, 60, 1954, p.86.

[12] T.J. Jenkin, 'The Expression of Welsh Farming', *Journal of the University College of Wales, Aberystwyth, Agricultural Society*, 24, 1932, pp.8–9.

[13] J. Sheail, 'Elements of Sustainable Agriculture; the UK experience, 1840–1940,' *Agricultural History Review*, 42, 1995, p.188.

[14] See, for example, R.J. Moore-Colyer, 'A Voice Clamouring in the Wilderness;

H.J. Massingham (1888–1952) and Rural England,' *Rural History*, 12, 2001, pp.85–108.

[15] R.J. Moore-Colyer, 'Homes Fit for Heroes and After; Housing in Rural Wales in the Early Twentieth Century', *Welsh History Review*, 24, 2009, pp.82–103.

[16] See M. Davies, *Save the last of the magic; Traditional qualities of the West Wales Cottage* (Llandysul, 1991). I am especially grateful to Mr David Frost, Senior Consultant with ADAS, Pwllpeiran for his comments on this section and his very valuable observations on a variety of aspects of this chapter.

[17] R.J. Moore-Colyer, 'Lighting the Land; Rural Electrification in Wales', *Welsh History Review*, 23, 2007, pp.72–92. By 1966 ninety four per cent of Welsh farms had mains electricity. However, there remained 1,200 farmers in some of the more far flung upland areas who were still not connected to the National Grid.

[18] S.M. Tibbott, 'Going Electric; the changing face of the rural kitchen in Wales, 1945–55', *Folk Life*, 1989–90, pp.64–72. As late as 1960 refrigerators were only to be found in 5 per cent of Welsh households (D. Kynaston, *Family Britain, 1951–57*, (London, 2009), p.618).

[19] See, J.L. Lees and R.J. Moore-Colyer, *Hill Farming in Wales; Manpower and Training Needs* (Agricultural Training Board, 1973).

[20] J.G. Williams, 'Changes in the Sheep Population of Wales', *Welsh Journal of Agriculture*, 8, 1932, pp.59–60.

[21] A wether is a castrated ram.

[22] E.L. Harry, 'Some Aspects of the Sheep Industry in Wales', *Welsh Journal of Agriculture*, 15, 1939, p.132.

[23] A.W. Ashby and J.R.E. Phillips, 'Some aspects of the Hill Sheep Farming in Wales', *Welsh Journal of Agriculture*, 2, 1926, p.40.

[24] A.W. Ashby, 'The Place of Cereal Growing in Welsh Agriculture', *Welsh Journal of Agriculture*, 17, 1943, p.74.

[25] W.H. Jones, 'Farm Productivity in Pembrokeshire', *Agriculture*, 60, 1954, p.344.

[26] J.A. Smith, 'The Production and Marketing of Market Garden Produce in the Aberystwyth area', *Welsh Journal of Agriculture*, 11, 1935, p.61.

[27] P. Atkins, 'The retail milk trade in London, *c.*1790–1914', *Economic History Review*, Ser. 2, 33, 1980, p.537.

[28] E.C. Crossley, 'A half century of dairying; from tradition to technology', *Journal of the Society of Dairy Technology*, 27, 1976, p.5; D. Taylor, 'Growth and structural change in the English Dairy Industry, 1860–1930', *Agricultural History Review*, 35, 1967, p.88.

[29] R.G. White, 'Cattle breeding and Dairying in Wales', *Journal of the University College of Wales, Aberystwyth, Agricultural Society*, 13, 1922, p.13.

[30] F.A. Barnes, 'Dairying on Anglesey', *Transactions of the Institute of British Geographers*, 21, 1955, pp.138–40.

[31] W. Jones and W. Cowie, 'Retailing of milk by producers in the Cardiff area', *Welsh Journal of Agriculture*, 10, 1934, p.82.

[32] J.R.E. Phillips, 'The Milk Marketing Scheme in Wales 1934–5', *Welsh Journal of Agriculture*, 2, 1936, p.97; S.B. Thomas, 'Some aspects of the graded milk movement in Wales', *Welsh Journal of Agriculture*, 8, 1934, p.214.

[33] There was a quantum increase after the war and machine numbers had reached 35,810 by 1956. For this and other statistics cited in this chapter, see John Williams, *Digest of Welsh Historical Statistics* (Welsh Office, 1985).

[34] D.J. Morgan, the County Agricultural Organiser for Cardiganshire reported in 1928 that his county, with 25 recorded herds, was at the forefront of the milk recording movement in Wales. The senior milk recorder for the county in the late 1920s was John Lewis MSc., who subsequently became Director of Dairying at the University College of Wales, Aberystwyth, a post which he held until his retirement in the 1970s. (R.J. Moore-Colyer, *Man's Proper Study*, (Llandysul, 1981)).

[35] J.D. Griffiths, 'The Changeover to Wartime Milk Production', *Welsh Journal of Agriculture*, 17, 1943, p.36.

[36] R.J. Moore-Colyer, 'Against the Odds; Grassland and Dairying in Wales between the Wars', *Journal of the Royal Agricultural of England*, 189, 1998, pp.203–14.

[37] *Cardigan and Tivy-side Advertiser*, 29 May 1929.

[38] R.J. Moore-Colyer, 'Horses and Equine Improvement in the Economy of Modern Wales', *Agricultural History Review*, 39, 1991, pp.126–42. On balance it seems that farmers showed more interest in equine improvement than in enhancing the quality of other farm stock.

[39] J. Davies, 'Horse labour on Welsh Farms, 1821–1927', *Welsh Journal of Agriculture*, 6, 1930, pp.46–7.

[40] D.W. Howell, *Taking Stock; The Centenary History of the Royal Welsh Agricultural Society* (Cardiff, 2003), p.81.

[41] Howell's assessment of farm income represented the margin between gross output and gross expenditure corrected for valuation changes. Expenditure on hired and family labour was included, together with a figure to take account of perquisites and the value of board and lodging *in lieu* of wages. A value was also attributed to the quantity of farm produce consumed in the house. In effect, farm income provided the reward to the farmer and his wife and return on capital employed.

[42] J.P. Howell, 'The Financial Results of different types of farms in Wales', *Welsh Journal of Agriculture*, 12–15, 1936–9, *passim*.

[43] Given that some 300 million eggs were consumed in Wales in 1930 relative to an output of 150 million, there was potential for further expansion, yet

this was resisted by many farmers who were unwilling to divert grain from other livestock to what they rather dismissively regarded as women's 'pin money'. (*Cardigan and Tivy-side Advertiser*, 8 August 1929).

[44] J.P. Howell, 'Economic Depression in Welsh Farming', *Welsh Journal of Agriculture*, 11, 1935, p.12.

Chapter 2

[1] K.A.H. Murray, *History of the Second World War; Agriculture* (London, 1955).

[2] J. Martin, 'The Structural Transformation of British Agriculture; the emergence of high input-high output farming', in B. Short, C. Watkins and J. Martin (eds), *The Front Line of Freedom; British Farming in the Second World War* (Exeter, 2006), p.17.

[3] P. Brassley, 'Wartime Productivity and Innovation, 1939–45', in Short, Watkins and Martin, (eds), *The Front Line of Freedom; British Farming in the Second World War* (Exeter, 2006), pp.53–4.

[4] J. Brown, *Farm Machinery, 1750–1945* (London, 1989), pp.80–2. For mechanisation as a whole during this period see, P. Dewey, *Iron Harvests of the Field; the making of Farm Machinery in Britain since 1800* (Lancaster, 2008).

[5] Ministry of Information, *Land at War; the Official Story of British Farming, 1939–1944* (London, 1945).

[6] B. Short, C. Watkins, W. Frost and P. Kinsman, *The National Farm Survey, 1941–3; State surveillance and the Countryside in England and Wales during the Second World War* (Wallingford, 2000), *passim*.

[7] R.J. Moore-Colyer, 'The County War Agricultural Executive Committees; the Welsh Experience, 1939–45', *Welsh History Review*, 22, 2006, p.162.

[8] *Cambrian News*, 31 May 1940.

[9] National Archives MAF 112/209; 80/5002. This seems a relatively rare survival, since neither the National Archives nor the Welsh Records Offices appear to have significant collections of Warag material.

[10] Moore-Colyer (Warags), op.cit., *passim*.

[11] *Cambrian News*, 7 August 1942; *Carmarthen Journal*, 13 June 1941.

[12] The *Admiral Graf Spee* was a famous German naval warship in the Second World War.

[13] R.J. Moore-Colyer, 'On the Home Front; Rural Life in Breconshire during the Second World War', *Brycheiniog*, XXXVIII, 2006, pp.85–102.

[14] R.J. Moore-Colyer, 'Prisoners of War and the struggle for food production; 1939–49' in *Front Line of Freedom*, p.118.

[15] R.J. Moore-Colyer, 'The Call to the Land; British and European Adult Voluntary Farm labour, 1939–49', *Rural History*, 17, 2006, pp.83–101.

[16] R.J. Moore-Colyer, 'Kids in the Corn; School Harvest camps and Labour Supply in England, 1940–1950', *Agricultural History Review*, 52, 2004, pp.183–206.

[17] R.J. Moore-Colyer, 'Keeping the Home Fires Burning; aspects of rural life in wartime Ceredigion, 1939–45', *Ceredigion*, XV, 2008. David Frost tells me that the autumn half-term holiday at Brynherbert School was referred to locally as 'Potato Week' until very recently. In a sad reflection of the changing rural demographic structure, the school is now closed and awaiting a buyer.

[18] For details see B. Short, C. Watkins, W. Frost and P. Kinsman, *The National Farm Survey, 1941–3; State surveillance and the Countryside in England and Wales during the Second World War* (Wallingford, 2000), *passim*.

[19] *Cambrian News*, 19 January 1940.

[20] A typical technical officer was Dr William Ellison, seconded from the University at Aberystwyth to the Montgomeryshire Warag. Ellison eventually became Professor of Agriculture at Aberystwyth until his death in 1977.

[21] See Moore-Colyer, 'The County War Agricultural Executive Committees', for further details. It is possible that the apparent lack of survival of Welsh Warag documents in the public domain is attributable to the reluctance of individuals to deposit what they regarded as sensitive material likely to promote controversy.

[22] National Archives, Ministry of Agriculture Fisheries and Food 112/219.

[23] Food intake in England and Wales averaged 2,923 calories per day over the war years. This compares with 2,000 calories in liberated Europe in 1945–7.

[24] Potatoes, in particular, were seen as a sort of national insurance against starvation and, like bread, were not rationed in Britain before 1946. By the summer of 1942, Germany had been forced to cut her potato ration by 50 per cent so that, as a matter of morale-boosting honour, it was felt vital that Britain maintain her supplies and grow and harvest the maximum acreage.

[25] A.W. Ashby, J.A. Smith and W.J. Thomas, 'Fertility and War Production on Welsh Farms', *Welsh Journal of Agriculture*, 8, 1943, p.5.

[26] J.D. Griffiths, 'The Changeover to wartime Milk Production', *Welsh Journal of Agriculture*, 17, 1944, p.35.

Chapter 3

[1] The word 'war' had been dropped from the title, and personnel and structures changed, yet the Committees retained many of their wartime functions and continued to influence local farming and farmers for more than a decade.

[2] For Tom Williams and the Labour government's role in farming see, C. Griffiths, *Labour and the Countryside; the Politics of Rural Britain, 1918–1939* (Cambridge, 2007).

[3] P. Brassley, 'Output and Technical Change in Twentieth Century British Agriculture', *Agricultural History Review*, 48, 2000, pp.60–89.

[4] A. Howkins, *The Death of Rural England; A Social History of the Countryside since 1900* (London, 2003), pp.152–3.

[5] D. Kynaston, *Austerity Britain, 1945–51* (London, 2007).

[6] C.J. Holmes, 'Science and the Farmer; the development of the Agricultural Advisory Service in England and Wales, 1900–1939', *Agricultural History Review*, 36, 1986, pp.77–86.

[7] The act also extended the scope of the Annual Price Review (est. 1945) to include some 80 per cent of gross agricultural output. The review was to become a yearly titanic struggle between the National Farmers Union negotiators and Ministry of Agriculture Fisheries and Food, as the two sides engaged, as Harold Macmillan put it, in discussions of 'Byzantine deviousness' (H. Macmillan, *Riding the Storm, 1956–9* (London, 1971), pp.23–4).

[8] A severe viral disease of rabbits that decimated the wild rabbit population when it arrived in Britain in the early 1950s.

[9] P. Brassley, 'Silage in Britain, 1880–1990; the delayed adoption of an innovation', *Agricultural History Review*, 46, 1996, pp.63–87.

[10] *Mid Wales Investigational Report of the Welsh Agricultural Land Sub-Commission* (HMSO, 1955, Cmd. 9631).

[11] Recovery was, however, to be short-lived in the face of the inexorable rise in capital intensive pig production. Sow numbers accordingly declined from 37,547 in 1966 to a mere 3,700 in 2006.

[12] The decision of the Milk Marketing Board to convert from churn to bulk collection in the mid-1960s effectively spelt the end for those small producers who could not afford to effect the improvements to roads and lanes necessary to cater for the new tankers. The consequences for the 'farming ladder' and the implications for the growth of the 'second home' market have yet to be properly studied. In any event, the relict churn stands at the end of many a farm lane in Wales are poignant reminders of the sometimes baleful consequences of technological change.

[13] See D.I. Bateman, 'Cardiganshire Agriculture in the Twentieth Century' in G.J. Jenkins and I.G. Jones (eds), *Cardiganshire County History III* (Cardiff, 1998).

[14] P. Midmore and R.J. Moore-Colyer, *Cherished Heartland: Future of the Uplands in Wales* (Cardiff, Institute of Welsh Affairs, 2005).

[15] It was widely alleged in the years prior to the 'capping' of headage payments, that rather too many farmers had used the often substantial sums involved to

purchase additional land, thereby to increase their stock numbers so as to be in a position to claim yet more headage payments. If the truth of this allegation is as yet unproven, it may well prove a subject worthy of study for historians of the future.

[16] The tourist industry in Wales claimed to be losing £10 million weekly at the end of March 2001. The fact that farmers received compensation for slaughtered animals during the outbreak, but small rural businesses were denied any financial recompense caused no little resentment.

[17] G.O. Hughes, 'ESAs in the context of a culturally-sensitive area', in M. Whitby (ed.), *Incentives for Countryside Management; the case of Environmentally Sensitive Areas* (Wallingford, 1994), pp.135–56.

[18] For details and references see, in particular, P. Conford, *Origins of the Organic Movement* (Edinburgh, 2001); R.J. Moore-Colyer, 'Towards Mother Earth; Organicism, the Right and the British Union of Fascists', *Journal of Contemporary History*, 39, 2004, pp.353–71.

[19] This was only exceeded elsewhere in the UK by the south-west of England at 9 per cent. (Figures from Organic Centre Wales.)

[20] R.J. Moore-Colyer and A.J. Scott, 'What Kind of Landscape do we want? Past, Present and Future Perspectives', *Landscape Research*, 30, 2005, pp.501–23.

[21] Oliver Goldsmith (1728–74), *The Deserted Village*.

Chapter 4

[1] R. Perren, *Agriculture in Depression, 1870–1940* (Cambridge, 1995).

[2] N. Goddard, 'The Development and Influence of Agricultural Periodicals and Newspapers, 1780–1880', *Agricultural History Review*, 31, 1983, p.123.

[3] For the general background see, R.J. Moore-Colyer, *Man's Proper Study; A History of Agricultural Science Education at Aberystwyth* (Llandysul, 1982), pp.1–16.

[4] A.O. Evans, 'Some Welsh Agricultural Writers', *Welsh Journal of Agriculture*, 8, 1932, pp.71–84.

[5] For details of the career of this remarkable man, who was involved in virtually all aspects of the development of Welsh agriculture for half a century, see, L. Phillips, 'Prominent Welsh Agriculturalists: Cadwaladr Bryner Jones, 1872– 1954', *Journal of the University College of Wales, Aberystwyth, Agricultural Society*, LX, 1979, pp.143–9.

[6] I.G Jones, *Explorations and Explanations; Essays in the Social History of Victorian Wales* (Llandysul, 1981), p.110.

[7] R.J. Moore-Colyer, 'Landowners, Farmers and language in the Nineteenth Century', in G.H. Jenkins (ed.), *The Welsh Language and its Social Domains, 1801–1911* (Cardiff, 2000), p.114.

[8] Very few indeed of the numerous sets of nineteenth or twentieth century farm accounts deposited in the National Library of Wales lend themselves to meaningful analysis. But there are probably valuable long-term runs of accounts lurking in the attics and storerooms of farmhouses around the country. One such set of diaries and accounts, covering in full the period 1915–57, was maintained by R.L. Jones of Penwenallt, Newcastle Emlyn, sometime Labour Officer for the Cardiganshire War Agricultural Executive Committee. Via the good offices of Mrs B. Jones of Aberarth, I have had the opportunity to study these rare and useful documents. Readers will appreciate that material of this sort is the very stuff of history and well worthy of preservation.

[9] E. Whetham, *Agricultural Economists in Britain, 1900–1940* (Oxford, 1981), p.20.

[10] P. Brassley in E.J.T. Collins (ed.), *The Agrarian History of England and Wales, VII, 1850–1914* (Cambridge, 2000), pp.606–7.

[11] E.H. Whetham, 'The Agriculture Act and its Repeal; the Great Betrayal', *Agricultural History Review*, 22, 1974, p.48; A.F. Cooper, 'Another look at the Great Betrayal; Agrarian Reformers and Agricultural Policy in Britain', *Agricultural History*, 60, 1986, pp.81–104; E.C. Penning-Rowsell, 'Who betrayed whom? Power and Politics in the 1920–21 Crisis', *Agricultural History Review*, 45, 1977, pp.176–95.

[12] For the period generally, see, P. Dewey, *British Agriculture in the First World War* (London, 1989); *Idem., War and Progress; Britain, 1914–45* (London, 1997).

[13] Brassley, Burchardt and Thompson, op.cit., p.167.

[14] *Third Report of the Development Commissioners*, 1913–14.

[15] See, for example, D. Hall, *A Pilgrimage of British Farming, 1910–12* (London, 1914), and C.S. Orwin and E.H. Whetham, *A History of British Agriculture, 1846–1914* (Newton Abbott, 1964).

[16] Whetham, *Agricultural Economists*, op.cit., p.66.

[17] M.K. Ashby, *Joseph Ashby of Tysoe, 1859–1919* (Cambridge, 1961), *passim*.

[18] D.I. Bateman, 'A.W. Ashby; an Assessment', *Journal of Agricultural Economics*, 31, 1980, pp.4–14.

[19] Obituary in *The Countryman*, Winter, 1953. Ashby's voluminous publications, sometimes written in conjunction with T. Lewis, J. Morgan Jones, J. Pryse Howell and others, emphasise his overriding concern with the *human* side of farming and with the village community, the integrity of the countryside and those living in it. Among the many essays published in *The Welsh Journal of Agriculture* in the 1920s and 1930s, titles such as 'The Human Side of the Farming Business', 'Human Motives in Farming' and 'The Social Origins of Welsh Farmers' underline this aspect of his work. He was equally concerned with the fortunes of the farm labourer and his family, hence, 'The Problem

and Position of the Farm Labourer in Wales', *International Labour Review*, XXXI (3), 1935; 'The Rural Standards of Living', *Welsh Housing and Development Association*, 1928 and 'The Sociological Background of Adult Education in Rural Districts', *British Institute of Adult Education*, No. 2, 1935. D.I. Bateman provides a full assessment of Ashby's academic work, while a complete collection of his writings (some 240 items) is held in the Thomas Parry Library at Aberystwyth University.

[20] J.S. Ashton, 'Some perspectives on agricultural economics', *Journal of Agricultural Economics*, 30, 1979, p.229.

[21] Whetham, *Agricultural Economists*, op.cit., p.57. The more recent steep decline in the number of agricultural economists in university departments of agriculture and the allied subjects may be attributed to a variety of factors. It is difficult, nevertheless, to escape the *feeling* that agricultural economics is no longer held in high regard in a subject area increasingly dominated by the molecular sciences.

[22] For details of appointments, see UCW Agricultural Committee minutes, November 1924–May 1934. Llefelys Davies would eventually occupy a senior position in the Milk Marketing Board, and J. Morgan Jones would become Registrar of the University at Aberystwyth between 1936 and 1944.

[23] The decision to build had been taken at the end of 1928 (UCW Staffing Committee minutes, 28 December 1928).

[24] Moore-Colyer, *Man's Proper Study*, op.cit., p.61.

[25] *A Survey of the Agricultural Departments of the University College of Wales* (Aberystwyth, 1937).

[26] Whetham, *Agricultural Economists*, op.cit., pp.91–2.

[27] J. Pryse Howell, *Agricultural Atlas of Wales* (Oxford, AERI, 1921); *Idem.*, *The Productivity of Hill Farming* (Oxford, 1922).

[28] J.P. Maxton, *The Survey Method of Research in Farm Economics* (London, 1929).

[29] *An Economic Survey of Agriculture in the Eastern Counties of England, 1931*, Farm Economics Branch Report No. 19, School of Agriculture, University of Cambridge.

[30] Their deliberations were published annually in the early volumes of the *Journal of Agricultural Economics*.

[31] A.W. Ashby, *Development and Situation of Research in Agricultural Economics in Great Britain, 1950* (Brugg, 1951).

Chapter 5

[1] J. Nix, 'Farm management; the state of the Art (or Science)', *Journal of Agricultural Economics*, 30, 1979, p.278.

[2] In all, 2,000 holdings in England and Wales provided data for the Survey.

[3] Funded initially by the Leicestershire philanthropist and cricket fanatic, Sir Julian Cahn, the scheme involved the reclamation of a large tract of derelict hill land. By utilising seed mixtures developed by the Plant Breeding Station and employing novel husbandry techniques, Stapledon and Griffith successfully pioneered a system of hill land improvement which would be adopted throughout Britain and elsewhere in the British Empire. The scheme formed part of a plan for the wholesale rehabilitation of the upland socio-economic environment embracing agriculture, forestry, housing and education, broadly similar to the vision set out in R.G Stapledon's remarkable, *The Land, Now and Tomorrow* (London, 1935). The symbolic and metaphorical aspects of the scheme were not lost on Welsh nationalists at the time.

[4] *Report on Research and Advisory Work in Agricultural Economics, 1937* (Department of Agricultural Economics, Aberystwyth, 1937).

[5] Aberystwyth University (AU) Archives, Principal's Correspondence, *Scientific and Secretarial Workers in the Department of Agricultural Economics*.

[6] Aberystwyth University Archives, Cabinet Office to Ashby, 4 June 1940.

[7] Ministry of Agriculture memorandum, EI, 739; Ser 416, 17 December 1940.

[8] Farms that, according to the Warag, were achieving less than 60 per cent of potential output.

[9] Ivor Evans (d. 1952) had a deep interest in agriculture and a wholehearted belief in the university's duty of outreach into the rural community. In addition to his Welsh publications, including a translation into Welsh of the *Fables* of La Fontaine, he collaborated with Ashby in *The Agriculture of Wales and Monmouthshire* (Cardiff, 1944).

[10] Recorders were appointed at the rate of one per 10,000 holdings for which each Centre was responsible and sometimes spent overnight periods in the towns where the district offices were located although, where feasible, a good deal of their work was undertaken by correspondence.

[11] The detailed organisation and operation of the Survey, involving hundreds of personnel throughout Wales and England, was extremely complex and is described at length in Short, et. al., *National Farm Survey*, op.cit., pp.41–79.

[12] *Nature*, 157, 1946, pp.364–5.

[13] G. McCrone and G.A. Attwood (eds), *Agricultural Policy in Britain; Selected Papers by E.F. Nash* (Cardiff, 1965). See also an obituary of Nash by the economist and civil servant, J.H. Kirk in *Nature*, 196, 1962, pp.1267–8.

[14] See his letter to Ruth Cohen quoted *in extenso* by Moore-Colyer, *Man's Proper Study*, op.cit. His 1959 memorandum on the future of the Department of Agricultural Economics and the proposal therein that closer links be forged with the Department of Economics expresses similar views.

[15] It became customary for much of the Survey and costings data to be used to form the basis of enterprise studies published in a series of volumes by the Department.

[16] Aberystwyth University Archives, Principal's Correspondence, 10 May 1946.

[17] Aberystwyth University Archives, Principal's Correspondence, Ivor Evans to J. Pryse Howell, 23 November 1946.

[18] Aberystwyth University Archives, Principal's Correspondence, Ministry of Agriculture to Ivor Evans, 24 January 1947.

[19] J. Winnifrith, *The Ministry of Agriculture, Fisheries and Food* (London, 1962), pp.217–18.

[20] Aberystwyth University Archives, R/DRS/AG/AG.ECON.

[21] Memorandum on the work of the Provincial Agricultural Economics Service, June 1956.

[22] Napolitan to Parry, 15 November 1960. Napolitan was profoundly interested in agricultural economics and extremely knowledgeable across the whole subject area. He was wont to sit through meetings of the Agricultural Economics Society in a deep and impressive silence. (I am obliged to Dr D.A.G. Green for this information.)

[23] Ministry of Agriculture, May 1959.

[24] Moore-Colyer, *Man's Proper Study*, op.cit., *passim*.

[25] Aberystwyth University Archives, Principal's correspondence, L. Napolitan to E.F. Nash, 15 November 1961.

[26] Aberystwyth University Council minutes, 24 June 1966. The move took them once again to the building on the Penglais site which they had originally occupied in the 1940s. This became the Stapledon Building and then the Cledwyn Building, the name it retains at the time of writing.

[27] D.I. Bateman, 'Professor H.T. Williams, C.B.E., F.R.Ag.S.', Journal of *Agricultural Economics*, 39, 1988, pp.477–8. After Nash's death, a move had been generated within the Department of Economics to absorb the agricultural economists into the new Faculty of Economic and Social Studies, which would have no departmental boundaries within it. This move, which would probably have been approved by Nash, was frustrated by the eventual appointment of Williams as head of an independent Department. In a sense, Williams's appointment might be seen as victory for those, including officials of the Ministry of Agriculture, who were keen to retain the idea of 'agriculture' within the discipline of agricultural economics.

[28] See R.J. Moore-Colyer, *Man's Proper Study*, op.cit., pp.135–8.

[29] Aberystwyth University Archives, Principal's Correspondence, Permanent Secretary, Ministry of Agriculture to Principal Thomas Parry, 20 July 1965.

Chapter 6

[1] Aberystwyth University *Reports to Council*, 1968–79. Additional funding was obtained from the Milk Marketing Board, the Welsh Agricultural Organisational Society and the University itself.

[2] Aberystwyth University *Reports to Council*, 1966.

[3] Initially the NAAS had tended to restrict its activities to scientific and technical advice. As time passed, however, the influence of Emrys (later Sir Emrys) Jones and other colleagues brought about a broad change of culture whereby advice came to be based upon a 'whole farm' approach, embracing both technical and business elements. In this context the economic and financial data gathered by the PAES was of vital importance to the quality of advice given. (I am obliged to Mr Edward Griffiths, formerly head of NAAS in Wales for his valuable observations on this subject.)

[4] Scion of a long line of Polish landowners, Jawetz was an extraordinarily forthright character, who, it has been alleged, was one of the last gentlemen in Europe to have squared up to his man in a duel of honour. (This tale was related to me by the late Professor Hugh Rees FRS, a close friend of Jawetz.) Jawetz left Aberystwyth for an overseas post in the early 1970s.

[5] The whole issue of Ministry funding was called into question in the 1980s. At the time both universities and government departments were faced with the need to cut costs and the Ministry of Agriculture began to query why it should be expected to pay for essentially academic posts. The potential loss of funding was deftly avoided at Aberystwyth by the simple tactic of arguing that anyone retiring from the Department did so from a Farm Management Survey post rather than a University funded academic one. (I am grateful to Emeritus Professor Michael Haines, sometime Director of the Welsh Institute of Rural Studies at Aberystwyth for this information.)

[6] Aberystwyth University *Reports to Council*, 1968 and 1979.

[7] I am grateful to Mr Rowland Davies, office manager of the FBS at Aberystwyth for his help with these details. Davies emphasised, in particular, the difficulties of locating farms in the pre-postcode days and the extent to which improvements to the roads over the past two decades have eased the lot of the investigational officer.

[8] The fact that farmers were getting their bookwork done free of charge was a further inducement, as was the acceptance by the authorities of accounts produced by the Survey as supporting material in grant and subsidy applications. (I am grateful to Mr David Williams of Trefenter for this observation.) Prior to joining the Survey as an investigational officer in 1974, Williams had been a schoolmaster and farmer and in the latter capacity had participated in the Survey. He testifies to the affection and respect with which the Survey and its officers were held throughout Wales and to the lifetime friendships forged between farmers and their local investigational officer. Throughout 20 years of visiting farms Williams claims never to have been

bitten by a dog. This distressing fate he avoided by carrying his folded papers from his car to the farmhouse in the 'trail' position thereby diverting the attention of any ill-intentioned canine away from his legs towards the carefully rolled bundle of papers!

9   As Rowland Davies noted, investigational officers in England tended to arrive at the farm and carry off the accounts for processing in the comfort of their offices. Their Welsh counterparts spent the best part of a day on the farm with their 'green books' and made the effort to know and understand their farmers.

10   It is today considered essential for investigational officers to have come from a farming background, or, at the very least, to have built up a sound practical understanding of the farming business.

11   M.B. Roberts, the senior investigational officer in the mid-1970s had no great enthusiasm for technology and it was only after intensive lobbying from David Williams that he grudgingly sanctioned the purchase of pocket calculators.

12   I am grateful to Mr Nigel Chapman for his help with this section. A graduate in agricultural economics, Chapman became a junior research officer in 1978, before becoming computer officer for the Survey.

13   There still are some farmers quite happily still using the green book to this day.

14   I am obliged to Mrs Judith Jones, for more than 30 years a clerical assistant in the PAES, for this information. Mrs Jones testifies to the lively communal spirit among the clerical staff who seem on balance to have worked hard and lived hard. Christmas parties were memorably bibulous affairs and among the most celebrated was the occasion when the sometimes austere Dyfri Jones performed the singular feat of dancing to the 'Hallelujah Chorus' from the *Messiah*.

15   University Grants Committee, *Report of the Sub Committee on the Teaching of Agricultural Economics in Universities*, May 1970.

16   Aberystwyth University Archives, Note on senior lectureship applications, H.T. Williams to Registrar, 18 January 1971.

17   Aberystwyth University Council minutes, 13 July 1977. Williams died in March 1988 at the age of 75. A reserved and unpretentious man with distaste for pomposity and self-aggrandisement, he had a touching concern for the underdog. (Bateman, Obit. *Journal of Agricultural Economics*, 39, 1988). I had the pleasure of spending many hours with him in his retirement and can testify to our mutual enjoyment of whiskey and cigarettes and his unerring and selfless generosity. He was extraordinarily popular with the Survey clerical staff whom he frequently entertained in his home, and had the capacity to inspire fierce loyalty among those close to him. At the same time he would not hesitate to censure those whom he believed not to be 'playing the game'. The member of staff who drove the Departmental Ford Prefect car to Holyhead on the way to his annual holiday in Ireland soon learned the roughness of his tongue, as did the investigational officer who used his farm visits to enhance his income by selling double glazing. G.O. Hughes, meanwhile, recalls being hauled over the coals for being away from the Department during the Christmas vacation.

When the Professor of Biochemistry seized the chance to occupy one of his department's rooms while Williams was in Australia, the latter's fury on his return was awesome to behold!

[18] Aberystwyth University *Report to Council*, 1981–2. One of the principal commissions of the late 1970s and early 1980s was the large scale Hill and Uplands Research Project under the direction of D.A.G. Green and Dyfri Jones. This massive Ministry-funded undertaking gave rise to many reports and in-house publications. In the final report, the authors examined the role of the Ministry of Agriculture in the hills and uplands and concluded that the former's efforts should be directed increasingly in the direction of socio-economic rather than upon strictly technical issues. Issued in 1983, the report was rejected by the Ministry which, at the time, was not prepared to accept this interpretation of its role. Given the policy developments of the past two decades, one might conclude that the Aberystwyth economists were somewhat ahead of their time.

[19] I am grateful to Mr G.O. Hughes for his valuable comments on this and other aspects of the Survey's importance.

[20] T.N. Jenkins, 'Enterprise Studies', in D.A.G. Green (ed.), *Welsh Studies in Agricultural Economics* (Department of Agricultural Economics, 1986). The several volumes in this short and useful series contain articles both from academic members of the Department and several officers involved directly with the Survey, including N.D.H. Chapman, N.C. Reeves and E.D. Williams.

[21] Haines and D.A.G. Green in particular, strove conscientiously to make Ministry contract work relevant to their academic activities by utilising Survey material for teaching purposes and wherever practicable involving investigational officers in student farm visits and courses in agricultural business management.

[22] The title of Provincial Agricultural Economist lapsed with the retirement of H.T. Williams. D.I. Bateman was not keen on the idea of Wales as a 'province' and when he did not adopt the title, the Provincial Agricultural Economics Service gave way to the Farm Management (and subsequently Business) Survey.

[23] Green was appointed senior lecturer in 1984 and retired in 1996. Besides producing the annual reports of the Survey, Green contributed significantly to the field of development economics, producing a considerable corpus of works on aspects of agrarian development in the Sudan, Ethiopia, Bangladesh and sub-Saharan Africa. Working with Dyfri Jones and others, he also wrote extensively on many aspects of the Welsh rural economy, sometimes drawing upon Survey data for the purpose. (I am particularly grateful to Dr Green for his many helpful comments on this chapter.)

[24] A party, hosted by Professor John McInerney, was held in Whitehall to celebrate the change. Green and Dyfri Jones attended.

[25] It has been suggested to me that the dictates of the Ministry were not *wholly* observed. Participating farmers as a rule did not wish to be dropped from the Survey and thereby to lose the considerable benefit of having their accounts drawn up in a clear and accurate form. Conversely, officers of the Survey were less than enthusiastic at the prospect of recruiting and training new participants, with all the effort that this involved. Given that the original sample had been to some extent self-selecting, there seemed little purpose in rejecting 50 farmers each year. Unofficially, then, some cooperating farmers remained in the sample for many years and the ministry *dictat* was transgressed "… to the benefit of everyone". (I am grateful to David Williams for this interesting observation.)

[26] V.W. McPherson, Welsh Office, to D.I. Bateman, 18 June 1993.

[27] Jenkins had been a senior research officer in the Department. His appointment by D.I. Bateman to the directorship of the FBS was part of a deliberate attempt to raise the academic status of the Survey and to encourage academic staff to embody Survey material in research publications. Bateman also took the view that the rapid developments in computerisation would ease the burden of the investigational officer's task and perhaps, in collaboration with other academic staff, enable he or she to generate publications based on Survey data. (I am grateful to Professor David Bateman for this and many other helpful observations.)

[28] Since one of these is an environmental economist, it might be more accurate to set the total at two!

[29] IGER was the offspring of the Welsh Plant Breeding Institute. In early 2008, the Institute of Biological, Environmental and Rural Sciences (IBERS) was formed by the merger of the Institutes of Biological Science and Rural Sciences, and the Institute of Grassland and Environmental Research (IGER) to create the UK's largest institute in its field.

[30] 'Farming Connect' is itself funded through the Rural Development Plan 2007–13, which in turn is financed by the EU Agricultural Fund for Rural Development and the Welsh Assembly Government.

[31] I am grateful to Mr Tony O'Regan for his kind assistance with the later sections of this chapter and readily acknowledge his passionate desire to celebrate the Survey's anniversary, one aspect of which was the commissioning of this publication.

Chapter 7

[1] For technical details of these changes see, T.N. Jenkins, *Financial Results from the Welsh Farm Management Survey, 1956/7–1980/1* (Department of Agricultural Economics, Aberystwyth University, 1982).

[2] J. Pryse Howell, 'Financial Results of Farms in Wales', *Welsh Journal of Agriculture*, 13–16, 1937–40; 19, 1945.

[3] These include the *Statistical Results*, produced annually by Aberystwyth University which replaced the *Farm Incomes in Wales* series initiated in the 1960s. The latter publications normally provide details of incomes alone whereas the *Statistical Results* offer a broad range of financial data and include details of enterprise gross margins.

[4] Net Farm Income is total farm enterprise output less total inputs (excluding the labour of farmer and spouse). In the Survey it is calculated as if all farms were tenanted and represents the return to the farmer and spouse for their labour and management. In order to reflect more recent developments in agricultural pluriactivity, the notion of farm business income has been lately adopted as the headline figure. This incorporates all sources of income from farm resources and represents the return to all unpaid labour and to all the capital invested in the farming business.

[5] The indices of inflation rates were based on L.H. Officer and S.H. Williamson, *Annual Inflation Rates in the United States, 1775–2009 and the United Kingdom, 1265–2009*, measuring worth 2009; http://www.measuringworth.com. I am obliged to Mr G.O. Hughes for his help and advice in compiling these figures.

[6] Between 1971 and 1976 net farm incomes in the United Kingdom as a whole grew by 9.5 per cent. On the other hand, arable farmers were the main beneficiaries, with livestock producers bearing the brunt of the general increase in cereal-based feedstuff prices over the period.

[7] Differing definitions of inter-year samples account for some differences between the Welsh Assembly statistics and those of the Survey. The Assembly results, moreover, are weighted according to numbers of farms within the different categories in the Agricultural Census, while those in the Survey are unweighted.

Chapter 8

[1] Among these might be included David Jenkins's masterly *The Agricultural Community in South Wales at the turn of the Twentieth Century* (Cardiff, 1971) and Alwyn D. Rees's, pioneering *Life in a Welsh Countryside* (Cardiff, 1950). D Parry-Jones's illuminating *Welsh Country Upbringing* (London, 1948) and *Welsh Country Characters* (London, 1950), like D.J. Williams's *Hen Dŷ Ffarm* (Aberystwyth, 1953) commemorate the world of west Wales in the earlier twentieth century, while Huw Evans's *Cwm Eithin* (Liverpool, 1950) evokes the countryside of north Wales a century ago. More recently, numerous studies utilising both documentary material and personal recollection lay bear some of the realities of rural life in twentieth century Wales, including for example, R. Phillips, *The Tredegar Estate, 1300–1956* (Upton-upon-Severn, 1990) and E. Rees (ed.), *Carmarthenshire Memories of the Twentieth Century* (Carmarthen, 2002).

[2] This chapter is based extensively upon interviews undertaken by the author and Dr Alun Davies, FBS investigational officer, with individuals whose farms

were included in the Farm Management Survey at various times and for varying periods after 1936.

[3] David Jenkins notes the careful social distinctions current in the Welsh farmhouse in the early twentieth century, while printed labour agreements for servants emphasise the meticulously observed social gradations in the rural community. (R.J. Moore-Colyer, 'Conditions of employment among the farm labour force in nineteenth-century Wales', *Llafur*, 3, 1982, pp.9–20.)

[4] Hubert Phillips notes that the prevailing spirit of cooperation began to evaporate as farms were sold to people from beyond the local area or beyond the borders of Wales. During his youth, Llanboidy and its environs were almost entirely Welsh speaking; today he has a single Welsh-speaking neighbour.

[5] www.bbc.co.uk/news/10510360

[6] See D. Linehan and P. Gruffudd, 'Unruly Topographies; citizenship and land settlement in inter-war Wales', *Transactions of the Institute of British Geographers*, 29, 2004.

[7] One of his first moves was to join the Farm Management Survey and Waunfawr remained a participating farm until the mid-1990s. Hubert found involvement with the Survey not only intrinsically interesting, but a potent stimulus to improve.

[8] Mr Nixon-Strong of Tŷ Mawr, Kidwelly, twice closed down by tuberculosis in recent years, speaks movingly of the anguish, uncertainty and stress of living from TB test to TB test. He has abandoned maize as a forage crop on the grounds of its attractiveness to badgers.

[9] W. Davies and J. Jones (eds), *The Poetical Works of Lewis Glyn Cothi* (London, 1837), pp.431–2. Aberbechan appears prominently in G.T. Hughes, P. Morgan and J.G. Thomas (eds), *Gregynog* (Cardiff, 1977).

[10] John Price recalls that his grandmother regularly walked to Newtown market hall with eggs and butter for sale, on her return selling food of various descriptions to soldiers stationed at the tank firing range on the western border of the farm.

[11] Although they are hosts less regularly these days. The dreary dictates of health and safety legislation, funding limitations and the absurd restrictions of an over-prescriptive curriculum have rather curtailed school visits in the last few years.

[12] The tradition was alive and well in the early twentieth century when many landed estates were being sold. When a non-local butcher attempted to outbid a sitting tenant during the sale of the Velinnewydd Estate at the Castle Hotel in Brecon in September 1919, he was dragged from the auction room and violently assaulted by a group of the tenant's kinsmen. Again, at the auction of the Camrose (Pembrokeshire) estate around the same time, tenants who had previously been sent notices to quit so as to ensure a freehold sale demonstrated their collective loyalty at the auction by refusing to bid for farms. (R.J. Moore-Colyer, 'Farming in Depression; Wales between the wars, 1919–1939', *Agricultural History Review*, 46, 1998, p.174.)

[13] www.muddymatches.co.uk/press-coverage/wp-content/uploads/2011/04/
finding-love-on-line.jpg

[14] Rural Stress Review, www.arthurrankcentre.org.uk/projects/rusource_
briefings/firm04/181.pdf; www.farmercrisisnetwork.org.uk/who

[15] John ap Hywel and others played an important role in the activities of the
Dyfed Action Group which sought to influence government policy towards
the difficult issue of milk quotas in the early 1980s. John himself, who had
been involved in student politics and campaigning on behalf of the Welsh
language, was well versed in civil disobedience and, together with various Plaid
Cymru politicians, spoke passionately on the milk quota issue both in Wales
and in England. At venues across the land, they expressed the profound depth
of feeling and resentment at the UK government's approach and Minister
of Agriculture Michael Jopling's application of EEC directives. Against the
objections of some farmers, John proposed that producers donate a day's milk
each week to the striking south Wales miners, desperate to retain their jobs
against the possibility of pit closures. This they did, and in so doing developed
a profound sense of fellow feeling and sympathy with the mining community.
This extraordinary example of group solidarity and of the preparedness of
working farmers to attempt actively to influence events and official attitudes
is deserving of more than a footnote in the agricultural history of twentieth-
century Wales when it is eventually written.

[16] Williams is a Cardiff-trained biochemist, ap Hywel a graduate in English
and American Studies from Aberystwyth and Jones studied at the Welsh
Agricultural College.

[17] M. Muggeridge, *The Thirties* (London, 1940), p.198. In interpreting this
quotation, I fear, it will be necessary to follow the well-trodden route, 'For
Wales, read England'.

[18] For details and further references for these paragraphs see, R.J. Moore-Colyer,
'From Great Wen to Toad Hall; Aspects of the Urban Rural Divide in Inter-
War Britain', *Rural History*, 10(1), 1999, pp.105–24.

Postscript

[1] E.L. Ellis, *The University College of Wales, Aberystwyth, 1872–1972* (Cardiff,
1972), p.27.

Index of Persons, Places and Institutions

Farming in Wales 1936–2011 is just one of
a whole range of publications from Y Lolfa.
For a full list of books currently in print, send
now for your free copy of our new full-colour
catalogue. Or simply surf into our website

www.ylolfa.com

for secure on-line ordering.

TALYBONT CEREDIGION CYMRU SY24 5HE
e-mail ylolfa@ylolfa.com
website www.ylolfa.com
phone (01970) 832 304
fax 832 782